THE CRISIS OF CAPTAINCY

THE CRISIS OF CAPTAINCY

Servant and Master in English Cricket

David Lemmon

CHRISTOPHER HELM
London

Christopher Helm (Publishers) Ltd, Imperial House,
21–25 North Street, Bromley, Kent BR1 1SD

ISBN 0–7470–2004–3

A CIP catalogue record for this book
is available from the British Library

Phototypeset by OPUS, Oxford
Printed and bound in Great Britain by
Butler and Tanner Ltd., Frome, Somerset.

Contents

List of Photographs

Prelude

On the afternoon of Tuesday, 10th June 1986, David Gower sat on the balcony at Lord's, a lonely figure amid a bustle of people. His hands clasped, his shoulders rounded, his eyes tired, the mood pensive, he exuded the air of a beaten man. He was the captain of England, and England had just lost to India at Lord's for the first time in a Test match. Moreover, it was England's sixth Test defeat in succession, and Gower had been the England captain in each of those defeats.

India's win at Lord's had been achieved by some purposeful and inspiring cricket, yet England had contributed much to their own downfall. Having scored 294, they had seen India reach 232 for 3, but had then taken five wickets for 32 runs to force themselves back into contention. When India's ninth wicket fell only nine runs separated the two sides, but Downton missed an easy stumping chance, Vengsarkar reached his century, and he and Maninder Singh added 38 to give India a first innings lead of 47. It was a lead which proved to be all important.

When India went in search of the 134 runs that they needed to win on the last day Gower was unable to call upon either Dilley or Emburey, both of whom were injured. Dilley had taken two quick wickets and sent a shiver of nervousness through the Indian side before he had been forced to retire. Emburey had been unable to bowl at all so that Gower was without both his main bowlers at the time he needed them most. These two absences and the missed stumping on the Saturday evening were factors beyond Gower's control, as was the inability of his batsmen to cope with the pace and unrestrained hostility of the West Indian fast bowlers in the Caribbean a few months earlier, but he had committed the unforgivable crime of leading England to six successive defeats, and as he sat and mused he was well aware of the punishment in store. Indeed, the press had given him ample warning of what to expect and had suggested that it should be administered forthwith.

Shortly after the end of the match at Lord's Gower was informed by the Chairman of the Test selectors, P.B.H. May, that he was being replaced as captain. He was not the first to suffer such a fate for failing to win a Test match.

Mike Gatting was named as Gower's successor, and there was an irony in the choice. Gatting had lost his place in the England side when West Indies won all five Tests in Gower's first series as England's captain, 1984. Gatting had been seized by a habit of offering no stroke to balls which were moving in to him and had twice been adjudged l.b.w. in such a manner in the Lord's Test match, the only appearance he made against West Indies in 1984.

He had been named as vice-captain to Gower, however, for the tour to India that winter and had blossomed and flourished as a Test batsman. He had contined to blossom when Gower led England triumphantly against Border's Australians in 1985, but, in the West Indies, he had suffered a badly broken nose early in the tour and had been forced to return to England. He had gone back to the Caribbean in time for the last Test in which he scored 15 and 1, but his absence from the first four matches of the series meant that he was exempted from the criticism that was levelled against most of his colleagues. With the possible exception of John Emburey, Gatting was the only Englishman to emerge from the series unscathed.

There were other ironies in his assumption of the England captaincy. He had arrived at the position almost by default, and he represented the re-establishment of the 'NCO' as leader as opposed to the 'officer and gentleman', typified, for some, by David Gower.

Gatting had arrived as captain of England after leading Middlesex with considerable success for just over three years. At Middlesex, he had inherited a fine side from Brearley who, during his tenure of the captaincy of the county, had had several vice-captains, Mike Smith, Phil Edmonds, John Emburey and Gatting himself among them.

Smith, an able and intelligent professional of long standing, had retired. Edmonds was an eccentric and an individualist who had not always enjoyed the smoothest of relationships with Brearley. Emburey, too, was something of an individualist in his approach to the game, but he had proved himself a thinking and perceptive cricketer. He was seen as a future captain of Middlesex, but his appearances in South Africa with the South African Breweries' team led by his friend Graham Gooch had cost him dear. He had suffered a three-year ban from Test cricket and had been deprived of the vice-captaincy of Middlesex, which had passed to Gatting. Gatting had been second in command when Brearley retired so had inherited the Middlesex captaincy, which placed him in a strong position to take over as England's leader. Middlesex were one of the two strongest and most successful counties in England, but Gatting's form in international cricket had never suggested a permanent place in the Test side. His appointment as vice-captain to Gower for the tour of England, 1984–5, was, in truth, against logic, but, as we have noted, he flourished on that tour, hitting his first Test century in what was his 54th Test innings. He prospered in the slaughter of Australia, avoided the carnage in the Caribbean through no fault of his own, and, with Gooch and Emburey having exempted themselves from consideration for the time being because of their South African escapade, he presented himself to the selectors as the only possible alternative to Gower as England's captain.

The dismissal of Gower came as no surprise. There had been sections of the press who had been advocating that his head should roll, and though many would like to think otherwise, the press exerts considerable influence on the thinking of the selectors. Yet many of those who were anxious for his removal from the England captaincy in 1986 were the same ones who had been adamant that he should replace Willis two years earlier.

The support for Gower had its foundations in the oldest of arguments. In the words of one journalist, a man of public-school background, Gower had been born to the job, trained for it from the day he was born. It was a question of pedigree.

Gower had been educated at King's School, Canterbury. His school record was in *Wisden*. He had gone from school to the University of London where, for a year, he read Law; but university life was not suited to him, and he joined Leicestershire to follow cricket as a profession.

Those who believed that they saw in Gower a return to the leadership of the Golden Age were deceived by appearances. They were seduced by the charm and elegance of the batting. The Adonis-like features and the public-school education suggested to some a return to Fry or Chapman or any of those handsome amateurs of the earlier part of the century for whom cricket appeared to be such an easy game and who were adept at so many sports and pastimes. Perhaps such atavism is part of a disease, the perpetual search for some golden age that is remembered only in the dreams of others and whose very historical existence is questionable. Certainly Gower is no reincarnation of an Edwardian spirit. He is essentially a child of our time. His ease of manner contrasts sharply with the haughty aristocracy of a Fry and the confident application of discipline. Gower was reared in an age which has fostered self-questioning and doubt.

To the victor the spoils. Gower holds aloft a miniature of the Ashes. Border and Peter West smile in congratulation. Gower's reign after this triumph was to be brief.

That doubt was never more manifest than in his attitude to captaincy. At the end of his reign as captain of England, he still declined invitations to talk or write on the question of leadership, yet others with less than half his experience have readily accepted the chance to present treatises on the subject.

Mike Gatting did not attend public school. He spent his secondary years at John Kelly Boys' High School in the London Borough of Brent. There was no question of a university education. He was destined to be a professional sportsman. There was no other calling. Only the choice between cricket and soccer presented itself, and he was on the Lord's ground staff at the age of 16.

Frances Edmonds, in a gentle passage in her book *Another Bloody Tour*, draws a perceptive distinction between the two men, Gower and Gatting:

> Poor David. Uneasy, indeed, lies the head that wears the crown. He looked so slim and frail and wispish, like a pedigree two-year-old filly, as he walked disconsolately back to his team-mates in the dressing-room. 'Gatt', on the contrary, is vaguely

> reminiscent of a shire horse. Strong, sturdy, reliable, unflappable, he walked out to the wicket swinging his bat, doing his little on-the-spot-running hops, and looking decidedly as if he at least, meant business.

The image is consistent with general conceptions of the two men and the contrasting values some would have them represent – the prospective Derby runner and the faithful workhorse; the gifted well-born amateur and the honest, hard-working professional; the man destined to lead because of his birth and schooling and the man destined to serve; the officer and the sergeant-major; the gentleman and the player.

In cricket, these artificial social divisions were abolished by legislation in 1963. In society, they are being eroded by the passage of time and by changes in emphases and in economic conditions, yet many preserve them in their hearts. They see the division and the acceptance that some are of a class shaped to lead by birth and breeding as part of a comforting tradition; but it is a tradition whose base is insubstantial and insecure, a tradition which has caused some of the game's uneasiest moments and greatest problems.

Gower is an uncharacteristic and unwilling example of the tradition that a 'gentleman' should captain. He is essentially a professional cricketer of the latter part of the 20th century, and would win a place in an England XI as one of the outstanding batsmen of his generation, irrespective of all other considerations. But it has not always been thus.

The tradition that an amateur should captain a side because of the assumption that his background and attitude made him fit to lead, while accepted by some, was rejected by others on the grounds that often the selected leader was not a good enough player to be in the side. Never was this more manifest than in the two All-India teams which toured England in the 1930s.

The 1932 side was led by the Maharajah of Porbandar. S.J. Southerton, in *Wisden*, explained the appointment and the situation with admirable tact.

> Some little difficulty was experienced with regard to the captaincy, and after one or two disappointments the choice fell upon the Maharajah of Porbandar who had with him as vice-captain K.S. Ganshyamsinhji of Limbdi. For reasons apart from cricket, the necessity existed of having a person of distinction and importance in India at the head of affairs, and it was almost entirely because of this that Porbandar led the team. No injustice is being done to him, therefore, by saying that, admirably fitted as he was in many respects for the task, his abilities as a cricketer were not

commensurate with the position he occupied. Only those, however, with intimate knowledge of the many little difficulties arising in the command of a body of men of mixed creeds, habits and thoughts, can appreciate the tact and firmness required in maintaining that comradeship and united endeavour so essential to the success of a team on the field and the harmonious collaboration of its various units in other respects. Except for his limitations as a cricketer, the Maharajah of Porbandar enjoyed in full measure the attributes necessary to his position, and he certainly created in the team an excellent spirit.

Of the vice-captain no mention is made, and neither captain nor vice-captain appeared in the Test match when the side was led by C.K. Nayudu, a most accomplished cricketer. Porbandar appeared in only four first-class matches on the tour, scoring two runs in three innings. He did not bowl. K.S. Ganshyamsinhji of Limbdi played in eleven games and averaged 9.62 from 17 innings. He also did not bowl.

The leader of the 1936 side, the Maharaj Sir Vijaya Vizianagram – he was knighted during the tour – received less sympathy from *Wisden*, although he 'carried far more cares and worries than are usually the lot of the captain of a touring team'.

'He did not accomplish anything out of the common in batting but could not alone be held responsible for the limited success of the side. Cricket is essentially a team game, and in a band of players divided amongst themselves the will to pull together was not often apparent.'

Vizianagram played in all three Tests, averaging 8.25 from his six innings with the help of two not outs. He did not bowl. He was virtually ever-present on the tour and hit 600 runs in 42 innings, but his main claim to fame was that, on the eve of the first Test match, he sent home the side's leading player, Lala Amarnath, for disciplinary reasons.

Vizianagram had not been the original choice as captain. The Nawab of Pataudi, a batsman who had accomplished much at Oxford and for Worcestershire and who had scored a century on his début for England against Australia, had returned to India and was the obvious choice as captain of the 1936 side, but a mixture of ill-health and political pressure forced him to stand down.

The Viceroy of India, Lord Willingdon, was a Cambridge blue and former Sussex player. He was a strong supporter of Vizianagram who was elected captain of the Indian party in Pataudi's place. Major R.J. Brittain-Jones, the Comptroller of Willingdon's Household, was named as manager of the side. There was no vice-captain and no selection committee.

However high his social standing and however strong the political influence of his supporters, Vizianagram was unfitted for his task, both as a cricketer and as a leader on the field. In seeking support within the team, he caused divisions, and by the time the tour was a month old, the Indian Press was running a 'Vizzy must go' campaign.

One can only conjecture at what the atmosphere within the side was like, but it was apparent that the more experienced and accomplished players had little respect for the captain who knew nothing of English conditions and had a scant knowledge of the game.

At Leicester, Amarnath had demonstrated his dismay and disapproval of the field-placings that his captain insisted upon, and he had been warned as to his 'attitude towards the captain and manager'. But he had scored a century against Northants and a century in each innings against Essex as well as being the leading bowler in the side. At Lord's, however, trouble erupted again.

A strong Minor Counties side made 286, and the Indians were 89 for 1 at the close. Play did not begin until 3.30 the next day, and Merchant and Mushtaq Ali extended their stand to 215. Amarnath had been down to bat at number four and had sat padded up throughout the stand which lasted, in all, for two hours 20 minutes. When Mushtaq Ali was out he prepared to take the field, but Vizianagram told him that he had changed the order. Amarnath finally went in with ten minutes remaining and five wickets down.

One not out at the end of play, he stormed back to the dressing-room, flung his bat and pads into a corner and loudly condemned the whole way in which the side was being led and the way in which he was being treated. The commotion disturbed MCC members in the room below the dressing-room. Lord Willingdon was either one of those members or was quickly made aware of what had happened. At 6.00 on the Friday evening, Major R.J. Brittain-Jones, the manager, ordered Amarnath to return to India the following morning. C.K. Nayudu, Wazir Ali and other senior members of the side pleaded on his behalf, and a letter of apology was drafted and given to Vizianagram who agreed to rescind his order. But he then said that the matter was in the hands of Brittain-Jones and that arrangements had been made and could not now be altered. On the Saturday morning, Amarnath was on his way back to India.

No explanation was offered for his dismissal, which seriously weakened the side, and when he arrived in his own country the Indian Board of Control wished to send him back to England, but Vizianagram and Brittain-Jones refused to have him.

That Lord Willingdon played a part in the affair was apparent. He made a speech attacking Amarnath and supporting Vizianagram at The Oval two days after the all-rounder's departure, and he was, after all, one who gave orders to Brittain-Jones and the one who had manipulated affairs to have Vizianagram named as captain.

The tour continued in bizarre fashion. The captain was accompanied by 36 items of personal luggage and two servants. He was born to the purple, a princely figure, and he looked it, but, as Edward Docker, historian of Indian cricket, pointed out:

> If only he could have played the game as well as he looked the part. But he was no cricketer, however much people in Britain tried to pretend that he was, even though his aggregate of runs at the end of the tour was 600, an average of 16.21 per innings. 'What did he expect me to do?' an English county captain complained after 'Vizzy' had presented him with a gold watch just before their match began. 'I gave him a full toss and a couple of long hops, but you can't go on bowling like that all day, not in England'.

There was a move by senior members of the side to have C.K. Nayudu or Wazir Ali made captain or at least to be consulted in selection. Merchant, a young batsman of outstanding talent, tried to persuade the captain to stand down from the second Test and allow C.K. Nayudu to lead the side, but the Maharaja Sir Vijaya Vizianagram continued to lead the side in every match and he and Brittain-Jones were despotic.

It is significant that when Vizianagram was absent, receiving his knighthood, the touring side, inspired by Merchant and skipper C.K. Nayudu, gained their first victory over a county. It is also significant that Amarnath, admittedly a rather lively and controversial character, played in all five unofficial 'Tests' against Lord Tennyson's side, 1937–8, and was later a captain of India and chairman of the selectors.

Porbandar had been a success in 1932 because he had come to terms with his own limitations as a player and had realised that his best work could be done as a non-playing captain, speaking for the side off the field and helping to cement individuals into a team. Vizianagram had no such humility, and he paid the price. He returned home to face a board of enquiry.

The report of this committee was not intended to be published, but a special meeting of the Indian Board voted that its findings should be made public, and they were published in the *Times of India* early in 1937. Of Vizianagram it was said, 'There was a strong feeling among most members of the team that he was not successful as a playing captain, and that he did not understand the placing of the field or the changing of the bowling and never maintained any regular order in batting.' It did not leave room for much else.

If we have tended to dwell on and emphasise the limitations of an Indian touring captain of the 1930s, it is because he is an enlarged representative of a tradition which had its roots firmly in England, the tradition that an amateur of distinguished social position and influence was, because he had those advantages, the ideal captain. He was used to commanding men and to being obeyed. He was not dependent on cricket for his living and was therefore able to take an objective view of a game and of the needs of the team above the individual performance. One presumes that the qualities which his team-mates found lacking in Vizianagram, the manipulation of bowlers, the setting of fields and the intelligent use of batting resources, were assumed to be inherent in those with the necessary education and social background, or that they simply did not matter when set alongside the greater qualities of authority and leadership that the right man brought to the job.

For more than 150 years writers on the game have striven to identify the virtues needed to captain a cricket team successfully. John Nyren, in his chronicle of the men of the great Hambledon Club at the end of the 18th century, tells of Richard Nyren, his father, as the famous village side's leader.

> He was the chosen General of all the matches, ordering and directing the whole. In such esteem did the brotherhood hold his experience and judgement, that he was uniformly consulted on all questions of law or precedent; and I never knew an exception to be taken against his opinion, or his decision to be reversed. I never saw a finer specimen of the thoroughbred old English yeoman than Richard Nyren. He was a good face-to-face, unflinching, uncompromising, independent man. He placed a full and just value upon the station he held in society, and he maintained it without insolence or assumption.

Writing 54 years after the publication of Nyren's *The Young Cricketer's Tutor*, Prince Ranjitsinhji considered, too, that 'For obvious reasons many of the qualities most desirable in a captain are the result of experience of cricket and the world'. Ranji believed that the natural gift for leadership was an inborn quality synonymous with strength of character, and that to captain a cricket team was simply to apply that strength of character to the game. He believed that something almost superhuman was needed to discharge the post fully, for the duties were various and complex, 'social, moral, intellectual and practical'. No one could fulfil the duties of a cricket captain adequately without being 'a good man and a good cricketer', by which he meant not being an outstanding player, but having a thorough understanding of the game and a sensitivity to its needs.

For Ranji, the social side of the game, the care of opponents, and the sporting spirit were all important, and he listed the qualities necessary in a good captain – tact, resource, readiness, decision, even temper, enthusiasm and the ability to inspire others. It was implicit in Ranji's thinking that such qualities could only be brought to fruition in the best schools and universities.

Less than a decade after Ranji's exposition of his theories on the game, A.E. Knight published *The Complete Cricketer* in which he echoed many of the Prince's thoughts. His passions regarding captaincy were unrestrained, and his prose took on a mellifluous quality when he touched upon the subject. He felt, 'The captain of a side should always . . . be a man to whom the rest of the side can look up with respect. His qualities as a cricketer should not be pressed too far.'

Like Nyren and Ranjitsinhji, Knight held that great captaincy came from richness of experience, outside as well as inside the game, yet Knight was aware that he was asking for an exceptional being.

> The great captain differs so deeply from the dull clay of ordinary men, that his infrequent presence is not to be wondered at. He is probably as rare an incarnation as the philosopher-statesman for whom Plato sighed. Qualities and powers rarely met in combination go to make him: an enthusiasm for the game; a sportsmanship of the highest order; a great knowledge of the game and of the conditions and environments which affect it; a greater knowledge of men and their methods, and an innate capacity for leadership; – such magnanimous gifts may not have been denied to angels, they have assuredly not been lavished upon men. A man of noble aims, yet of intensely practical character, is, moreover, obliged to frame his schemes in accordance with the quality of the agents supplied to him.

Pelham Warner, too, placed enthusiasm as the most necessary of attributes for a captain.

> The ideal captain must possess a sound knowledge of the game, a cool judgement, tact, and, above everything else, enthusiasm – for enthusiasm is a quality which enriches life and gives it zest, and the man who is enthusiastic about his eleven and their doings will, unless his influence and authority are sapped by disloyalty and want of co-operation, soon inspire the same feelings of zeal for the common cause in his followers.

In characteristically more down to earth and contemporary terms, Ray Illingworth emphasised much the same necessary virtues all had done since Ranji. 'One word sums up a successful cricket captain: versatile. He needs the patience of a saint, the diplomacy of an ambassador, the compassion of a social worker and the skin of a rhino. Boundless enthusiasm, the insight of a psychologist and the smooth-talking style of a con-man might also come in handy.'

Mike Brearley, the most successful England skipper after the departure of Illingworth, is far less glib in his assessment of the qualities most necessary to a captain. His treatise on the subject, *The Art of Captaincy*, won renown and a wide readership, yet he really narrows down the attributes needed by the successful captain to two broad categories – how well he knows the game, and how well he is able to motivate others.

Brearley was unique among modern captains in that, for much of the time that he was leading England, he was not a good enough batsman to be in the side; but so successful was he as a leader of men that he retained his place. In essence, Brearley fits neatly into the tradition of the amateur captain, public school, university, a life not dependent upon the game, but, paradoxically, it is a tradition he rejects. 'Birth, breeding, superficial attractiveness are dangerous grounds on which to select a leader. Yet for almost a century England and the counties restricted their choice of captains to a small percentage of those who play first-class cricket.'

That they did so was because the system was accepted by all. In 1906, Albert Knight could write:

> Our captain is an enthusiast who has kindly consented to undertake that most onerous and honourable position. We are glad that he is an amateur, because in the interests of pure sport we think it preferable for the ruling genius of a team to be one apart from the paid player, and one, in a financial sense, independent of the governing committee. A captain in such a position, who can command the respect of his team apart from his official character, is ideally situated. Not that one shares for a moment the unfair assumption that a professional player is inevitably a poor or an indifferent captain. So few professional players have been or are permanent captains of a team that the assumption seems rather gratuitous. It is simply impossible under the social conditions of present-day cricket for a professional to be fairly considered as a captain.

And so it was to remain for more than half a century to come. Knight himself was a professional, but he was one, by reason of the social climate in which he lived, who doffed his cap to the amateur, and he believed that amateurs infused a spirit different from that of the professionals and that they should be encouraged and included in a side even if they were inferior players to the professional whom, on occasions, they replaced.

2 The Legacy

The social divisions that existed in cricket were, as Knight intimated, simply a mirror of the way in which society itself was structured. Wherever and however cricket had its origins, by the time it began to be shaped and formulated into something resembling the game we know today, it owed much to the patronage of the nobility and a wealthy middle class.

Although it is likely that there were earlier drafts of laws of the game, the first known code of conduct was the *Articles of Agreement* drawn up to cover the matches played between sides raised by the Duke of Richmond and sides raised by Mr Broderick of Peperharrow in 1727. That rules to govern the game and behaviour were necessary was due in part to the fact that victory was not only prestigious, but financially rewarding as, initially, large sums of money were bet on the outcome of matches and substantial purses offered as prizes. It was the gentry who laid large wagers on matches, and it was they who employed professional cricketers to give strength to their sides.

A man's ability at cricket could win him employment on a wealthy estate where he would, in all probability, carry out a variety of tasks; but it was his expertise with bat and ball which were his greatest assets in the summer months. In his book, *English Cricket*, Christopher Brookes argues that one of the reasons that the aristocracy became so involved in cricket was that it gave them a chance to come into contact with a large cross-section of people employed on their estates and, by their presence, to impose greater authority over them. However good the professionals employed, they would invariably give way to their social superiors when it came to captaining the cricket team. Richard Nyren may have been the 'general', but Lord Tankerville led Hambledon in their victory over England in 1777.

Lord Tankerville was a leading patron of Surrey while John Sackville, third Earl of Dorset, was mainly associated with Kent. It was said that the Earl of Dorset spent £1,000 a year in keeping a group of professionals to aid him in his various encounters. Certainly gentlemen who ran large estates and established cricket teams engaged professionals to assist them late into the 19th century.

In the mid-19th century, at The Auberies, on the Essex-Suffolk border, Captain Caledon Alexander, noted in racing circles, ran a highly successful side and, at various times, employed William Lillywhite, John Wisden, Alfred Diver and William Caffyn as professionals. In his memoirs, Caffyn tells how he would play a cornet solo for the entertainment of the gentry as they sat at dinner in the evening after a match. Their stations in life already decreed that the gentleman and the player should change and eat in different places, yet it is worth recalling the assertion of one of England's great historians, G.M. Trevelyan, who, in his *English Social History*, maintained: 'If the French *noblesse* had been capable of playing cricket with their peasants, their châteaux would never have been burnt.'

Certainly there seems to be no evidence that the early English professional bore any grudge against those who employed him, quite the reverse, in fact; while the English nobility themselves were convinced that they were carrying out a great social function with their matches and bringing joy to the peasants.

The President of I Zingari wrote to the members of the Club in 1848 to the effect that the spread of cricket was a panacea for the ills of the kingdom.

> Hear again that happy laugh ringing from yonder group of sturdy peasants, in triumph of the downfall of the wicket of some opponent of their lord. It is not the excited laugh of revelry and dissipation issuing from the poverty-stricken frequenters of the beer-house; it is the genuine offspring of esteem and affection begotten in the service of a master who sympathizes with his lowly brethren, softens their trials, and welcomes them to share in his pleasures and amusements. Oh! that such sympathy were more universal!

I Zingari had been formed as a wandering club some three years before this letter was written. At a dinner in Bond Street following a match at Harrow, a group of friends had conceived the idea of forming a club of exclusively amateur cricketers who should undertake all the tasks of a match without the assistance of hired professionals to bolster the bowling.

To bowl was the main function of the professional. MCC, founded in 1787 and soon established as the most prestigious club in terms of tone-setting and law-making, employed practice bowlers, and by 1836 had as many as ten on the staff at Lord's. Their principal duty was to bowl to the members who came to practise, and so a pattern emerged of amateurs batting and professionals bowling. In their early years, the all amateur I Zingari side suffered several defeats because of the paucity of their attack. More significantly, the encounters between the Gentlemen and the Players which began on the original Lord's ground in Dorset Square in 1806 often saw the Gentlemen strengthened by the inclusion of professional bowlers. Beldham and Lambert assisted them in the first match, Howard and Matthews over the next few years, and in 1827, the Gentlemen fielded 17 men against the Players' eleven and still lost the second match by an innings.

Such imbalance suggested a situation ripe for exploitation, and the entrepreneur emerged in the shape of a shrewd Nottinghamshire professional, William Clarke.

The north was a professional stronghold. In the 19th century and, indeed, up until the First World War, only two counties, Nottinghamshire and Yorkshire, officially appointed professional captains. William Clarke, who led Notts from 1835 to 1855, was the first of them.

Born in 1808, Clarke was a bricklayer by trade, but he later became a publican, becoming landlord of the Trent Bridge Inn in 1838 and laying out a cricket ground alongside it. He had lost an eye before he was 30, but it did not affect his cricketing prowess. As a bowler he was supreme. He bowled under-arm, delivering the ball from just above hip level, turning it sharply from leg and achieving considerable bounce from the pitch. He made an intelligent assessment of his opponents, watching them at practice and set his field accordingly. In the matter of specialised field-placing to trap certain batsmen, he was a pioneer, but he was a pioneer in much else.

In 1846, he founded the All-England XI. He gathered together the finest cricketers of his time and, under his management and captaincy, they toured the length and breadth of the country. They played local sides, mostly against the odds, and drew large crowds. Not all of his side were professionals, but they were all paid a reasonable sum.

Fuller Pilch, for example, had played as a professional in Norfolk, where he was born, Suffolk and Yorkshire before moving to Kent. Initially, there was insufficient work for a man to earn a living just as a cricket professional, and Pilch was not alone in trying his hand at other trades and falling heavily into debt. Clarke's All-England XI offered Pilch and others full professional employment as cricketers, work for up to six days a week and a standard wage. In fact, Clarke was the first to offer cricket as a professional alternative to lower paid and more menial tasks which many had been forced to undertake.

What Clarke's side also did was to spread interest and enthusiasm for the game far and wide, encouraging a local fervour which was to find its ultimate outlet in the county game. Few men have made a greater impact on the game than Clarke, and it was his successor, George Parr of Nottinghamshire, who took the first English team on tour, to North America in 1859, while the second English team to tour, Stephenson's to Australia two years later, was also an all-professional side.

Clarke's All-England XI became disunited in 1852 because the captain-organiser had grown dictatorial and greedy. The amount of travelling involved in fulfilling the ambitious fixture list was immense, and many of the young players felt that the payment of £4 to £6 a match was insufficient, especially as Clarke himself was known to pocket as much as £40 on occasions. Wisden and others formed the United England XI in 1852 and swore that they would never play with or against a side in which Clarke had any involvement. A further fracture brought about the United South of England XI, but by then disagreements had become common. Money was a dominant factor.

The second English side to tour abroad, Stephenson's side in Australia, 1861–62, was to have been led by George Parr; but he and other northern professionals rejected the terms that were offered, which was why H.H. Stephenson of Surrey was given the task of selecting the side. Stephenson, one of the first recipients of a hat for taking three wickets with successive balls, invited six Surrey men, two Yorkshiremen and one from each of Middlesex, Sussex and Kent to accompany him. Parr and other northern professional players responded by stating that they would play no matches at The Oval or at any other southern ground.

The professionals had grown in power and prestige and their power was bringing about considerable changes in the game, changes which those who held authority, like MCC, were slow to administer. It should not be imagined that the professionals were leading some political revolution. It was economic, and social only in as much as all economic changes have social implications. More than anything it was an example of that self-help which was so dear to Victorian hearts.

MCC reasserted its authority by taking responsibility for the amendments to laws which changes in practice had brought about. The England XI would play the United England XI at Lord's at Whitsuntide for the benefit of the Cricketers' Fund, an embryo county championship came into being in 1864 and the same year, following the match between MCC and Oxford University at Lord's, a meeting was held in the tennis court at which over-arm bowling was legalised. A vexed question had been settled.

If the amateur establishment had regained its authority in the legislature of the game, those same amateurs still awaited a champion who would reassert their authority on the field. In 1853, at Lord's, the Gentlemen had gained a surprise victory over the Players, but from that point until 1865, the Players won 19 of the 20 encounters and the other was drawn.

When, at Lord's in 1865, the Gentlemen at last reversed the trend they had in their side W.G. Grace. Six feet tall and not yet 17 years old, he and his brother E.M. played a significant part in the victory. W.G. was to bestride the fixture like a Colossus for the remainder of the century, and the Gentlemen's superiority was to be as marked as the Players' had been in the period before the coming of Grace.

For 20 years a line of professional bowlers had dominated the game, and, as Bernard Darwin wrote, 'Generally speaking it was the amateur's part – and an amateur then simply meant a gentleman – to find the money, and to back his side rather than to play for it.' W.G. Grace changed all that as he changed so much else. In the first place, he killed the professional fast bowling of the 1860s. This was never better exemplified than in July 1869, when he went to Bramall Lane, Sheffield, and, playing for the South against the North, was 99 not out at lunch on the first day. Against the all professional attack of Freeman, Wootton, Emmett and Iddison, on a fiery wicket, he hit 122 out of 197. He followed this with six wickets, and the South, with five amateurs in their side, won by 66 runs.

As a batsman Grace was far superior to any man who had preceded him. As a bowler he was as thoughtful and cunning as Clarke had been, studying the weaknesses of his opponents and setting fields accordingly. As a fielder he had no equal in his younger days. In short, he quickly established himself as the greatest all-round cricketer that the game has known. Moreover, he was a gigantic personality whose presence was to draw large crowds and even increase the admission charge.

His ascendancy came at the time when county cricket was being shaped into something resembling the game we know today. Middlesex, Lancashire and Yorkshire were among those counties founded in the 1860s. Gloucestershire, under Grace, formally came into being in 1871, and within two years they were the leading county.

Grace's dominance of cricket made him the most famous Englishman of his age, and, with Charles Dickens, the most popular. The two men evoked a similar response. They stirred memories of a time which, if it had ever been, had passed, but, simultaneously, they asserted Victorian values. To a society which was becoming increasingly urbanised, Grace brought the taste of country pursuits,

W.G. Grace.

but he blended it with a hard-headed business acumen which his contemporaries understood and respected.

He was uninhibited in his approach to cricket and to life. His supreme confidence was drawn from his mastery as a player and his authority from this and from the certainty of his middle class. He, more than any other man, re-established the amateur as the leader in cricket, but there were other influences.

The Walker brothers of Southgate, who derived their wealth from their brewery, had been responsible for the foundation of Middlesex in 1864, and the metropolitan county was predominantly amateur for the first 50 years of its existence. Several other counties followed a similar pattern, and only Nottinghamshire, until 1889, and Yorkshire, until 1883, were led by professionals.

It was no easy task for a professional to manage a team of fellow professionals even if, like George Parr, who succeeded Clarke as captain of the All-England XI and led Notts until 1870, he had the advantage of being something above the rest of his side in social position. The financial aspirations of members of the team were always a problem, as were the clashes of personality and temperament in a side of 'equals'. The prime example was to be found in the disbanding of Cambridgeshire in 1869. The county had been among the strongest in the land for five years, but it was torn apart by the lack of discipline among its band of talented professionals.

Cricket, however, was becoming a more structured and ordered game. Rules were drawn up to govern qualification to play in the county championship in 1873, and the championship itself was formally structured in 1890.

There was a greater competitive sense in county matches than ever before, and in the same era, Test matches began to prosper. England's side in what was later called the first Test match, March 1877, was an all-professional one, but two years later, it was the 'Gentlemen' of England, with Ulyett and Emmett, who played at Melbourne under the captaincy of Lord Harris. Lord Harris was captain again in the first Test match to be played in England, at the Oval, 1880. This game saw W.G. Grace's debut in Test cricket, and he hit England's first-ever Test hundred.

If Grace helped to reassert the tradition of amateur captaincy, he also brought to the game a ruthless professionalism. In 1878, he abducted William Midwinter from the Australian party in order that he should play for Gloucestershire. Midwinter was born in Gloucestershire, but had emigrated to Australia and played for them in the first Test match, but he returned to England and played with Grace who contracted him to assist the county of his birth during the 1878 season. The Australians arrived that year with eleven players, believing that Midwinter would make their party up to twelve. He played for the Australians in their opening matches and was practising at Lord's just before the game against Middlesex when Grace arrived and insisted that he should be playing for Gloucestershire.

He bundled Midwinter into his carriage and drove him across London to The Oval where Gloucestershire were playing Surrey. Conway, the Australian manager, gave chase and a heated argument took place outside The Oval. Grace was strong in his language to the Australians and later apologised, but he won his point. Midwinter played for Gloucestershire for the remainder of the season and indeed for the five seasons after that.

The struggle over Midwinter and the rivalry with the Australians did much to rekindle Grace's fire for the game, for he had been suggesting that he might have to retire from the game to concentrate on his medical work and his family commitments. He did not retire, and he bestrode the game for another quarter of a century.

He dominated the matches in which he played not only by his expertise, but by the strength of his personality. He chattered endlessly on the field and had the reputation of being able to sway the opinions of umpires. Above all, he was aware of his own position in society and in relation to the game of cricket. He was an amateur because of that status. He was a gentleman, but that did not prevent him from making money from the game to which he gave so much. He was the recipient of a national testimonial to which the *Daily Telegraph* alone donated £5,000 which they had raised by means of a shilling subscription. In short, he knew the value of his standing in the game.

His friend Charles Green who shared some heroic partnerships with him for MCC and the Gentlemen asked him to come to Leyton to bring prestige to the first match of importance at the ground. Green had played for Middlesex, but he was an Essex man who, more than any other, drove that county into the first-class game. Grace stayed with Green for some days and was entertained regally, even being given the use of one of Green's finest horses. After he returned to the West Country Grace wrote to his old friend thanking him warmly for his hospitality, but he added that he would like to receive 20 guineas for the advertisement he had afforded the new ground at Leyton by his presence there.

In 1896, in the third Test match at The Oval, when Grace led England to victory in the series, five of the English professionals threatened to go on strike before the match because of an argument over fees. Their grievance was that the amount that they were being offered was poor in comparison to the large sums that the 'amateurs' received for playing. Abel, Hayward and Richardson relented and played, but Gunn and Lohmann refused to play.

The Surrey Club felt it necessary to make an official statement on the matter, and they professed that Dr Grace had never received more than ten pounds for a match, and that sum had to cover his travel from the West Country and his stay in London. The general reaction of the public was that the Champion was being insufficiently rewarded for the part he was playing in the game.

Grace was amateur in spirit, but professional in application, and it was this combination that gave the Victorian gentlemen renewed vigour and confirmed their authority as the leaders and law-makers of the game.

Captain of the first Test side in which Grace appeared was Lord Harris of Kent. The county had long been recognised as one of the cradles of the game, but the Club formed in 1859 was of a limited nature, and a substantial reorganisation took place in 1870, bringing into existence the County Club we know today. Initially without a regular captain, Kent appointed Lord Harris as skipper in 1875, and he remained in charge for 14 years. His reign only came to an end when he went out to India to become Governor of Bombay. This did not end his connection with the game, however, for he was later President of Kent and of MCC and held a commanding position in cricket until his death in 1932.

Lord Harris was rigid in his application of the Laws. He rooted out the bowlers whose actions were illegal and maintained strict rules on qualification. He revived Kent cricket, emphasised the amateur as the controller of the game for its own good, gave authority and credibility to MCC as cricket's governing body, and worked hard on behalf of the professional cricketer, assured of his social superiority over them.

Lord Harris was autocratic and did not suffer fools gladly, characteristics he shared with Grace and with his friend Lord Hawke. Like Harris, Hawke was educated at Eton, but he went on to Cambridge while Harris went to Oxford. His career followed the pattern of Harris's career in other respects – he organised England sides to tour abroad, and he was President of Yorkshire, his county, as well as President of MCC. If Harris revived Kent cricket, Lord Hawke created Yorkshire and took them to a position of total dominance among counties. He led the side for 28 years, and, under his leadership, they won the Championship eight times. To defeat Yorkshire when Hawke was the county captain was one of the richest prizes in the game, but it was not accomplished too often once he had got the side into shape. If Grace reasserted the strength of the amateur and the amateur spirit, it was Hawke who, in most minds, offered the incontrovertible proof of why a gentleman should captain a county.

As the Hon. M.B. Hawke, still at Cambridge, he won a place in the Yorkshire side, until then a totally professional one, and in 1883, he was appointed captain. He was quick to realise that he had at his command a team of immense talent, but equally quick to realise that they needed sympathetic management and strong leadership. He provided both.

Lord Harris – Captain of Kent and England, and a dominant personality in the game.

The Yorkshire professionals were, for the most part, hard-drinking, with little sense of county pride. Lord Hawke imposed a discipline which guaranteed a better lot for the professional as a reward for stricter application to his work. He saw Peate as a trouble-maker, unruly in his attitude; consequently, the great slow left-arm bowler's career was ended in 1886, although he was still highly successful. With customary tact, *Wisden* suggested, 'Without using a harsh word, it may fairly be said that he would have lasted longer if he had ordered his life more carefully.'

The career of Robert Peel, another of Yorkshire's great slow left-arm bowlers, was ended in an even more dramatic manner eleven years later. At Bramall Lane, in 1897, he arrived at the ground much under the influence of drink. His colleagues attempted to avoid catastrophe by reporting to his Lordship that Peel was indisposed and that the twelfth man should take the field in his place. Unsuspecting, Hawke agreed, but when Yorkshire took the field twelve men appeared and one of them was Peel. He expressed his readiness to bowl, but he proposed to do so at the pavilion rather than at the stumps, and he urinated on the outfield. He was ordered off the field, and Lord Hawke's judgment meant that he was never to play for Yorkshire again.

Hawke ruled on the field and in the committee room, and his voice was strong in the council chambers of cricket long after he had ceased to play. He stated later that Peel never bore him any grudge, nor argued with his banishment. What Hawke did, he did for the good of cricket and of Yorkshire.

The view of the professional cricketer as being one who was a likeable fellow, but most definitely in need of guidance and discipline is echoed in a *Times* leader of 1882:

> He is generally a capital fellow, whose only failing is to spend improvidently what he earns easily. It is no small temptation to a mere youth, emerging suddenly from local celebrity, to find himself overloaded with admiration and paid on a handsome scale. That his head is seldom turned with praise, and that his success does not very often sink him in dissipation, speaks well for the general manliness and healthy character of the class. The cricket professional is more deserving than most of those who minister to human pleasure. It is only lamentable to think that the goal of his aspiration is, too frequently, to be the proprietor of a public house.

Lord Hawke, of course, was to earn lasting fame, or notoriety, for a remark he made at the Yorkshire Annual General Meeting in 1925. In replying to a vote of thanks, he said: 'Pray God, no professional shall ever captain England. I love and admire them all but we have always had an amateur skipper and when the day comes when we shall have no more amateurs captaining England it will be a thousand pities.'

It has been customary to quote the first sentence and omit the remainder, and to use Hawke's remark to prove that he was a Blimp condemning, with horror, one faction of the human race. This was not

Lord Hawke – the father of Yorkshire cricket.

the case. Lord Hawke, like Lord Harris, did much for the professional cricketer and was respected for it. Many sought his counsel. But Hawke and Harris were men born to a social position which placed upon them, as they saw it, a responsibility which they never shirked. Their attitudes and assumptions have, for the most part, become outmoded through the fighting of two world wars and the move towards a more egalitarian society, but they should not be judged by the doctrines and philosophies of the late twentieth century.

Grace, Harris and Hawke lived at a time when social divisions were more readily accepted than they are today. They were men shaped on the grand scale. Grace would lunch on roast beef and a large hunk of cheese. He was always most careful to see that the catering was right, and the hock and claret were plentiful. He also enjoyed his favourite drink, whisky and seltzer.

In the 1870s, the early days of county cricket, the mid-day break in a game was more generally referred to as a 'dinner break', for the amateurs would often leave the ground and wine and dine heartily at a good hotel nearby. The amateurs and professionals generally changed in different dressing-rooms and took the field through different gates. When they were on tour they stayed in different hotels. In the press and on score-cards, the amateurs were referred to as Mr, the professionals simply by their names.

These distinctions were observed and accepted without question, for Grace, by outstanding ability and strength of personality, and Harris and Hawke, by the authority of their birth and social positions, had asserted the right of the amateur to lead. This was one of their legacies to the game, but by the generations that followed it was only half-understood. Harris and Hawke could command not simply because they were gentlemen, but also because they were good cricketers with a thorough knowledge of the game and an intelligent perception of the needs of the moment. Not all of those who followed them were to be so blessed.

3 Business Commitments and the Golden Age

W.G. Grace's England career ended in 1899. He was within two months of his 51st birthday and had led England in the first of a five-match Test series against Australia. The selectors, who were the leading amateurs in the side under the chairmanship of Lord Hawke, met for lunch or dinner at the Sports Club and, as there were many of them, debated long. C.B. Fry, who had only made the side for the first Test at the insistence of W.G. Grace and had immediately been co-opted on to the selection committee, arrived late, and the Old Man immediately asked him whether or not Archie MacLaren should be in the side at Lord's for the second Test. MacLaren had scored heavily with Stoddart's team in Australia the previous winter, and Fry believed that he should play.

Grace, hearing Fry's reply, said that that settled it and he would resign from the England eleven. Evidently, he himself felt that the time had come for him to stand down as he was no longer as sprightly in the field as once he had been. Fry and others tried to dissuade him, but he was adamant. The surprise was that MacLaren came into the side as captain, no one having seemed to notice that F.S. Jackson was, in fact, senior to him.

Jackson, however, was not captain of Yorkshire for whom he made infrequent appearances, but MacLaren was captain of Lancashire. The year was to be Grace's last as captain of Gloucestershire as well as his last as captain of England. He had lost his daughter in 1898 and spent much time with his wife consoling her in their great loss. Midway through the 1899 season, the Gloucestershire committee unwisely badgered him to make his future intentions clear, and he resigned to become manager-captain of the London County Club at Crystal Palace, saying that he had 'the greatest affection for the

J.R. Mason, all-round athlete, captain of Kent, influential in high places.

county of my birth, but for the Committee as a body, the greatest contempt'. The venture at Crystal Palace was not to be the happiest part of Grace's career.

What is interesting to note is who were the captains of the other 14 first-class counties during Grace's last season with Gloucestershire and England.

Lord Hawke was still in charge at Yorkshire, and, as we have mentioned, MacLaren was captain of Lancashire. J.R. Mason had taken over at Kent. He hit 34 centuries in his first-class career and played in five Tests. E.G. Wynyard of Hampshire was also a capable batsman and Test cricketer while Gregor MacGregor, the Middlesex captain, was a fine all-round sportsman, a brilliant wicket-keeper who played eight times for England. Sammy Woods of Somerset, a violent all-rounder, played for both Australia, the country of his birth, and England, as did W.L. Murdoch of Sussex who had led Australia on four tours to England and appeared in 19 Test matches, one of them for his adopted country. He dropped out midway through the 1899 season, and Ranjitsinhji, one of the most delicately delightful batsmen the world has known, led Sussex in his absence. H.K. Foster, one of a famous brotherhood and a most able cricketer who could not give as much time to the game as many would have liked, was captain of Worcestershire, and John Dixon and Herbert Bainbridge, batsmen of above average county standard, were leaders of Nottinghamshire and Warwickshire respectively. Surrey were in the hands of K.J. Key, later Sir Kingsmill Key, who scored over 13,000 first-class runs and was known as 'a man of most original views, an always philosophic cricketer, and an imperturbable captain'. H.G.P. Owen, once a fine batsman but now ageing, was captain of Essex, and Sir Samuel Hill-Wood and C.E. de Trafford were the skippers of Derbyshire and Leicestershire.

Hill-Wood later became renowned as Chairman of Arsenal, and he and de Trafford are the only ones in the list whose career records might suggest that their qualities as cricketers were not sufficient to earn them regular places in county teams. Yet even this is deceptive, for both were widely respected and both commanded very weak sides.

By the outbreak of the First World War, the situation had changed considerably. Only four county captains, Pelham Warner, J.W.H.T. Douglas, F.R. Foster and A.O. Jones, had Test experience, and five of the other twelve were, arguably, not really good enough for first-class cricket. Neither are there substantial arguments to suggest that their captaincy compensated for their inadequacies as players.

In 1904, A.G. Steel, an all-round cricketer of distinction, wrote in *Cricket, the Badminton Library*:

> It is a strange fact connected with cricket that a good captain is but seldom met with. The game has made such progress in popularity during the last thirty years, and the numbers of those who are proficient in its different branches have increased so enormously, that we should certainly expect to find in our county and other important matches captains who thoroughly understand the duties

> they are called upon to fulfil. But on looking round we are disappointed to find that the really good captains in first-class (including of course county) cricket are extremely few, and these few are amateurs. The cause of this may be that few men are able to take part in first-class cricket after they have served such an apprenticeship as would give them the experience, calmness, and judgement necessary for the difficult post of captain; or it may be that the qualifications for a good leader in the cricket-field are, from their very nature, seldom met with – in other words, that a captain is born not made, and very seldom born, too. Few professional cricketers (it is a well-known fact) make good captains; we have hardly seen a match played where a professional cricketer was captain of either side, in which he was not guilty of some very palpable blunders.

Steel is uncompromising in his criticisms. The professionals are dismissed because they are too vulnerable to the wishes and murmurings of their colleagues, and only Shaw, Shrewsbury and Gunn are exempt. The captaincy of the Australian side before the advent of Murdoch is castigated on the grounds that 'It is in adversity at cricket, as in the more serious walks of life, that the best qualities come to the fore; and whenever the Australian bowlers were collared, the whole team seemed to go to pieces.'

'Amateurs always have made,' asserts Steel, 'and always will make, the best captains; and this is only natural. An educated mind, with a logical power of reasoning, will always treat every subject better than one comparatively untaught.'

The significant point about Steel's somewhat uninhibited condemnation of the quality of captaincy in England is that it was written at the height of what we have come to regard as The Golden Age, and among those captaining county sides at the time were Fane, Jessop, MacLaren, Jones, Woods, Fry, H.K. Foster and Lord Hawke.

In the decade up to 1905, the England batting was predominantly amateur, yet few of these amateurs could give themselves regularly to the game. Hon. F.S. Jackson, one of the greatest all-rounders the game had known, was rarely available for Yorkshire. He played only twice for them in 1906 although he had captained England in all five Tests against Australia the previous summer. R.H. Spooner, whose batting was one of the greatest glories of the Golden Age, was, through military service and other commitments, lost to cricket for three seasons. The demands of the Church on Gillingham and the Army on A.J. Turner deprived Essex of two cricketers of quality, while J.F. Byrne, the Warwickshire captain, could play in only half the county's fixtures in 1906.

The pattern is repeated endlessly. Whatever picture later generations have conjured of a leisured class able to devote their lives exclusively to sport, the reality was very different. The number of men whose income and freedom from business worries or commitments allowed them to play throughout the season was few. The result, in terms of captaincy, was bizarre. The by now accepted tradition that an amateur must lead the side meant that gentlemen who had played only a handful of first-class matches found themselves commanding a team of hardened professionals when the regular captain was absent. That the side was held together was due in part to respect for the system and primarily through the strength of an experienced and tactful senior professional.

Harry Lee, who appeared for Middlesex before and after the First World War, tells how J.T. Hearne, as senior professional, was in charge of the paid players when on tour. With the amateurs staying at a separate hotel, it was Hearne's duty to see that set hours for meals and bed were adhered to, and he ruled the professionals with iron discipline. None dared be late for a meal; none dared appear improperly dressed. In essence, it was the extension of a feudal system which they had learned and accepted as ground staff boys.

There were times, however, when even the good sense and maturity of players of the calibre of Hayward, Abel and Hobbs could not save a side from its self-inflicted wounds. In 1904, following the resignation of Livingstone Walker, Surrey had no regular captain. H.B. Chinnery, never able to play regularly, led the side in May, but he could not be induced to continue. In the following weeks, the side was led by an assortment of amateurs including H.D.G. Leveson-Gower, Lord Dalmeny (later Lord Rosebery), K.J. Key, returning in his 40th year, and J.E. Raphael, who was 22 and had played one match for the County the previous season. Not surprisingly, Surrey did not enjoy a good season.

They also endured troubles in 1909 when the Committee were in dispute with some of their professionals. Marshal was suspended and Rushby was left out of the side to meet the Australians. J.N. Crawford, a brilliant young all-rounder, was to be captain in that match, but he refused to play on the grounds that several essential players had been omitted. Crawford's stand in defence of the professionals had no precedent, and he and Surrey parted company. He took a teaching post in Australia, but returned after the war when the quarrel was patched up.

The non-availability of amateurs had a marked effect not only upon the fortunes of counties, but also on the composition of the England side. C.B. Fry and S.F. Jackson were the type of men who are the despair of us lesser mortals in that they were accomplished in practically everything to which they turned their hand. Fry was an

England soccer international, held the world long-jump record, played for Southampton in the 1902 Cup Final, edited a magazine, wrote books, stood as a Liberal candidate, was India's representative at the League of Nations and declined the offer to become King of Albania. Jackson served in the Boer War, became an M.P. and Financial Secretary to the War Office, was Chairman of the Unionist Party, Governor of Bengal and became a scratch golfer after learning the game by standing in front of a mirror practising shots he had learned from a book for the whole of one winter. Neither could give their whole time to cricket, yet both remained powerful men and both captained England. Fry led Sussex for four and a half seasons, but Jackson captained Yorkshire only on occasions. Although they played in 26 and 20 Tests respectively, neither of them could spare the time to go to Australia.

Coming down from Oxford, Fry made his Test debut with Lord Hawke's side in South Africa in 1896, but his remaining 24 tests, his last being in 1912, were all in England. Jackson's Test career lasted from 1893 until 1905, his *annus mirabilis* when he led England to victory by two matches to nil, and all his international appearances were against Australia in England. R.H. Spooner, the other gem of the Golden Age whom we have mentioned, played ten Tests between 1905 and 1912 and these, too, were all in England.

If Fry, Jackson and Spooner could not give their time fully to the game, others benefited from their absence. Pelham Warner came down from Oxford in 1896 with the intention of entering the legal profession, but an allowance from his mother and his income from journalism allied to other sources, allowed him to give his time wholly to cricket which was the total love of his life.

Lord Hawke invited him to go with his side to South Africa, 1898–99, and he captained England in Australia, 1903–04, and in South Africa, 1905–06, although he was not appointed captain of Middlesex until 1908 and played only three Tests in England, against Australia in 1909 and twice in the Triangular Tournament of 1912. He was not captain of the side on any of these occasions. Warner's Test career owed much to the fact that he was the amateur ready, willing and available to tour. He won the captaincy of the side to tour Australia, 1911–12, almost by default.

C.B. Fry was named as captain of the side, and Warner, R.H. Spooner and F.R. Foster were the other amateurs in the first eight men chosen for the party. Spooner was unable to accept the invitation, and Fry, having been responsible for selecting the side with Lord Harris, Lord Hawke and J.R. Mason, announced in August that he, too, would be unable to make the trip. Gilbert Jessop also declined so that the party was left with only three amateurs, Warner, who had

Pelham Warner's career ended romantically as he led Middlesex to the Championship on the final afternoon of the season, 1920. He continued to have a great influence on the game as an administrator.

now been named as captain, F.R. Foster and J.W.H.T. Douglas. Foster was the captain of Warwickshire, who had just won the County Championship, and Douglas was captain of Essex. Both men had captained their counties for only one season.

Douglas owed his selection to his performance in the Gentlemen and Players match at Lord's. It is hard for younger followers of the game to realise how important a part this fixture played in the cricket calendar. It was the contest between the best of the amateurs and the best of the professionals, something in the nature of a Test trial some seasons and the highlight of the year at other times when there was no touring side. Since Grace's heyday, the Professionals had generally held the upper hand, but, at Lord's in 1911, the Gentlemen won by 130 runs. Douglas hit 72 and 22 not out and took 5 for 53 and 2 for 38. It was the only occasion during the season when he took five wickets in an innings, but the occasion had enough importance to earn him an invitation to tour Australia.

J.W.H.T. Douglas, like Fry, was an all-round sportsman. Educated at Felsted School, he had excelled in all he turned to. He played soccer for England in an amateur international and he won the Gold Medal in the 1908 Olympic Games for the Middleweight Boxing Tournament. He was not, like Fry, a natural athlete, and all he accomplished was brought about by dedication and relentless hard work.

He first played for Essex in 1901, the year he left Felsted, but he was raw, and it was only after a couple of seasons with Grace's London County side that he began to establish himself in the Essex side. By the standards of his time, he was an obdurate batsman who became obsessed with defence in his later years, but by any standards, he was a fast-medium bowler of quality with a late swing which could trouble the very best.

F.L. Lane had captained Essex from 1904 to 1906, and he was succeeded by the colourful Charlie McGahey whose qualities were not really shaped for leadership. The County's financial position was precarious, and it was felt that a change of captaincy would help to reinvigorate the Club all round. It was contemplated offering the captaincy again to Charles Kortright, but he intimated that he was too old and seconded A.P. Lucas's proposal that Douglas should be captain. The appointment came as a great shock, for most had believed that P.A. Perrin would be offered the captaincy.

Perrin was one of the best amateur batsmen never to play for England. He had an astute knowledge of the game and was a fine judge of a player. He was 35. Douglas was 29 and no more, at the time, than a promising all-rounder. There were, however, other considerations, mostly financial ones.

As has been intimated, Essex's financial position in 1911, as for many years before, was precarious. Douglas's father, J.H., was a wealthy timber merchant, desperately ambitious for his son with whom he was very close. The accepted story is that old Douglas 'pulled a few strings' and helped the County out of their financial predicament on the understanding that his son would be captain. There may also have been a faction who believed that there was a shyness and lack of grace in Perrin which made him unsuitable as a captain. Whatever the reason, J.W.H.T. Douglas was named as captain of Essex and held the position until 1928. Only Grace and Hawke have led a county side for a longer period.

The third amateur in Warner's side to go to Australia, 1911–12, was Frank Rowbotham Foster. A right-handed batsman and fast-medium left-arm bowler, he had succeeded H.J. Goodwin as captain of Warwickshire at the beginning of the 1911 season. He was only 22 years old, but had already made his mark as a fine all-rounder and completed the 'double' in his first year as Warwickshire skipper.

His predecessor, Harold Goodwin, had won a reputation for the example of enthusiasm which he set, but as he played in only ten of the 20 county matches, it was hard to assess what value he was to Warwickshire who finished 1910 with only two counties below them in the championship table. Under Foster, Warwickshire won the title.

The party of 16 that set sail for Australia contained only three amateurs, which was unusual, but, as we have shown, not all were as fortunate as Douglas in having a father who was willing and able to allow his business to support his son's and his own cricket interests.

The amateur spirit pervaded the arrangements for the tour, for it was left to Warner and Tom Pawley, the manager, to thrash out the agreements on conditions of play and other matters when they arrived in Adelaide.

Warner began the tour with a century and then fell ill. He was not to play again in Australia. The MCC, who at that time had control of overseas tours, had given Warner autocratic powers. There was no vice-captain for the tour, no selection committee, such was the trust in senior amateurs. Warner, on his sick bed, had to decide to whom he was to hand over the staff of authority. He chose Douglas. Hobbs, Barnes, Rhodes and Gunn, senior cricketers, all of whom had toured Australia before, as had Strudwick, did not come into consideration as they were professionals. These senior professionals had, in fact, played 66 Test matches between them at a time when Tests were a rarer event than they are to-day. Neither Douglas nor Foster had played in a Test match.

Warner's choice lay simply between Foster and Douglas, and he reasoned:

> Both were county captains of the same standing, both having been appointed to their positions at the beginning of the summer of 1911. Foster had a particularly good record, having in his first season led Warwickshire to the top of the tree, but Douglas had done well with Essex, and was senior both in age and in cricketing experience, having played for Essex long before Foster appeared for Warwickshire, and having represented the Gentlemen against the Players at Lord's as far back as 1907.

J.W.H.T. Douglas. History has not treated him kindly.

> It would have been unfair, then, to have passed over Douglas, and my choice, therefore, fell on him.

Douglas was accused of a tactical error in the first Test, which England lost, in bowling four overs himself before handing the ball to Barnes, but, under his captaincy, England won the next four to sweep to an unparalleled triumph. Douglas himself bowled splendidly in the series as did Foster and Barnes.

A captain returning from Australia where his side had won 4 – 1 could be forgiven for thinking that he would lead his country in the forthcoming series, or at least be in the side, but that was not the way in the Golden Age.

Warner inferred that Douglas's bowling form had been such that, on returning to England, he might well be considered for the Test side when there was a full complement of players available. As it transpired, the selection committee met and C.B. Fry was appointed captain for the Triangular Tournament. The committee then disbanded, and Fry had autonomy for the rest of the summer. Warner was chosen for the first two matches of the six that England played in the competition, and Douglas played only in the last, against Australia at The Oval when he came in as a late replacement for Hayes of Surrey and did not bowl in the match.

In 1913–14, MCC were sending a side to South Africa where England had lost the previous series by three Tests to two. Warner, 40 years old, did not feel fit enough to lead the side. Fry and Foster were not available. F.L. Fane, who had not captained Essex for seven years, was approached to captain the side, but later Jessop said he would be available, and Lord Harris and his selection committee were pleased to offer him the leadership with Fane serving under him. Three other amateurs, M.C. Bird of Surrey, D.C. Robinson, the Gloucestershire wicket-keeper, and the Hon. Lionel Tennyson of Hampshire, accepted invitations to tour. Then Fane said that he felt he could neither tour nor return to Test cricket. Jessop also said that he now found that he was unable to go to South Africa. There was only one man who had the time and the financial support of his father and his company to make it possible for him to tour South Africa and captain the side, and that was J.W.H.T. Douglas.

England won four of the five Test matches, the other being drawn. S.F. Barnes played in the first four Tests and dominated the series by taking 49 wickets. Douglas had a splendid all-round tour.

Had Douglas's Test career ended at that point, he would have had a record as England captain which would have stood as second to none. He had played in eleven Tests, nine of which had been won. He had been captain in ten of those Tests, had won eight of them, drawn one and suffered defeat only in his first.

Later events have tended to diminish his achievement, and cricket historians, most of them from the ranks of former amateur cricketers, have been less than kind to him. He was not a great tactician, nor a great intellect, but he was savagely dedicated to the game and ruthless in determination and application. He gave one hundred and twenty per cent and expected all others to do as much.

He was criticised for his treatment of Barnes in the first Test in which he played, yet until his death Barnes was a staunch supporter of Douglas under whom he took 83 Test wickets. Hobbs and Sutcliffe, too, had the greatest admiration for him which they were ever ready to express, and for E.J. 'Tiger' Smith, the Warwickshire and England wicket-keeper, there was no better captain nor man. Nearly 70 years later, Smith was to say in the autobiography he dictated to Pat Murphy, '. . . where Warner always wanted the pros to look up to him and to let them realize he was boss, Johnny was as straight as a gunbarrel. There was none of this "Mr Douglas" nonsense with him. He let you know where you stood with him. He was one of us, more of a professional amateur than an amateur professional of the old school.'

This was a perceptive comment and could lead us to a reason why Douglas was done less than justice.

In the years after the First World War, the demarcation line between amateur and professional was still a strong one. Harry Lee, to whose experiences with Middlesex we have already referred, tells how, in 1923, he was called up before a sub-committee at Lord's which was investigating an incident at Canterbury. Lord Harris was in the chair and A.J. Webbe, the former Middlesex captain and then President, was present at the enquiry.

Having answered Harris's questions with some nervousness, Lee was relieved to hear his President say:

> 'That's a very good answer. I see exactly what you mean, Harry.'
>
> Lord Harris's eyebrows rose as dangerously as a short bumper on a fast wicket.
>
> 'Harry?' he said. '*Harry*?'
>
> 'Why, yes,' said Mr Webbe. 'Harry's one of *our* men.'
>
> 'Very well,' said Lord Harris, who seemed to feel that discipline had been strained to its limits. 'Very well, *Lee*. That will do.'

Lord Harris was a champion of the professional, but he was not a violator of the barrier that separated him from them. Whether or not Douglas was frowned upon for familiarity with professionals we do not know. It is highly unlikely, for he was a rigid disciplinarian and did not suffer fools gladly. He also had the habit of testing people when he first met them to see if they came up to standard. The fact remains, however, that many who were quick to damn him as a bad captain when his side began to lose matches were less inclined to praise him for the string of successes the England side had had under him.

There had been only thirteen players in the party that Douglas had taken to South Africa, and he stated afterwards that he would not tour in future with less than fifteen players, of whom at least five should be amateurs.

The amateur tradition flourished even though more and more of them could give less time to first-class cricket. There was the continuing belief that it was they who brought flair to the game, and there was sufficient evidence in Edwardian cricket to support this contention; and it was they, therefore, who would provide the dash and imagination, as well as the breeding, necessary to lead. But were the men who combined the qualities necessary in a leader with sufficient ability to play the game at first-class level in abundant supply? We have already noted that, by the time of the outbreak of the First World War, the answer to this question was 'no'.

Lord Hawke retired as captain of Yorkshire in 1910. He was 50 years old, and his appearance had become less frequent before his retirement. His work for the game was to continue unabated. He was responsible for getting winter pay for the professionals and for suggesting the introduction of selection committees, but his playing days, of necessity, were at an end.

In his last years, Lord Hawke had, to all intents and purposes, shared the captaincy of Yorkshire with Everard Joseph Radcliffe, 'Pink' Radcliffe, who was later to be knighted. Neither Radcliffe, nor Sir Archibald White who took over from Radcliffe in 1912 would have claimed they were worthy of a place in a county side. Both stepped forward because Yorkshire needed a captain, it was decreed that that captain must be an amateur, and they were the only men available to do the job. Radcliffe's career batting average was 10.86, and he also took two wickets; White averaged 14.32 and he did not bowl. Both owed much to the advice of their senior professionals. Radcliffe was not even a Yorkshireman, having been born in Devon, but then, come to that, neither was Lord Hawke who was born in Gainsborough, Lincolnshire. Yorkshire had wanted a man born in the county to succeed Hawke, for by now they had become strict about the subject, but the man whom they sought declined. That they offered the captaincy to him at all shows the somewhat extraordinary lengths to which counties were reduced in order to maintain the tradition of the amateur captain.

Albert Guy Pawson was educated at Winchester and played for Oxford in the Varsity match for the first time in 1908. He was to gain his blue all four years at university although, in his first year, the award came about in a rather strange manner. Druce Brandt had kept wicket in the Varsity match in 1907 and was still in residence when Pawson went up to Oxford. When Worcestershire came to play the University in June 1908, they arrived without a wicket-keeper. A.G. Pawson was asked to assist them.

The University were routed by Simpson-Hayward, the famous lob bowler, to whom Pawson kept magnificently, making three stumpings He later took a catch off Arnold and enjoyed an excellent match. The outcome was that he displaced Brandt in the Oxford side and kept for the next four years.

Pawson had been born in Bramley, and when Yorkshire learned this they invited him to play in a few games and keep wicket with a view to taking over the captaincy. David Hunter, the Yorkshire wicket-keeper, retired in 1909, and his successor, Arthur Dolphin, had yet to establish himself so that the arrival of Pawson would have suited Yorkshire well, but the Oxford blue decided to follow his career in the Sudan Civil Service. His single guest appearance for Worcestershire remained his one and only for a county.

Between the Acts

The Golden Age of cricket was brought to an end by the carnage of the First World War. The extent of the trauma that the soul of mankind suffered in those years between 1914 and 1918 was not immediately apprehended. Where there had been the horizontal divisions of class, there became, after 1916, a vertical division between those who had witnessed the horrors of the Western Front and those who had not. The wounds were so deep, the scars so painful, that those who were to record the agonies of the war years – Somerset Maugham, R.C. Sherriff, Remarque, Graves and the rest – could not do so until a decade had passed. For the time being it was accepted that there had been a war which would end all wars, and that the land fit for heroes to live in would recapture the leisured spirit and seemingly perpetual sunshine of the Edwardian period; yet first cricket, like all else, had to count the cost. Raphael, Blythe, Hutchings and Booth were among those who did not return, and there was a host of young officers who might well have led counties on the cricket field who fell in France and Belgium.

For cricket, the order seemed to remain as it had been. Yet, in retrospect, we can see that many significant changes date from that time. The dominance of the amateur on the field was at an end. Between 1919 and 1962, the year of the last fixture, the Gentlemen beat the Players at Lord's on only three occasions, 1934, 1938 and 1953. They had won four times at Headquarters in the ten years up to 1914.

Of the county captains in charge at the outbreak of war, only Baggally (Derbyshire), Douglas (Essex), Troughton (Kent), Wood (Leicestershire), Warner (Middlesex) and Wilkinson (Surrey) returned to lead their sides in 1919. Baggally, in fact, could appear in only three matches, and Chapman, who had led Derbyshire before the war, took over. Baggally's career with Derbyshire encompassed only 31 matches between 1912 and 1919, and his career average was 11.86.

Of the new county captains in 1919, John Daniell of Somerset was the most experienced. An inspiring fielder, he had led the County from 1908 to 1912 and contributed much to Somerset cricket. F.G. Robinson of Gloucestershire, H.L. Wilson of Sussex, G.W. Stephens of Warwickshire, Lionel Tennyson of Hampshire and D.C.F. Burton, Cambridge University and Yorkshire, were competent cricketers who had played Championship cricket in the years before the war. A.W. Carr was a fine batsman who was to lead both Nottinghamshire and England with distinction. But the most interesting appointments among the county captains in 1919 were Myles Kenyon of Lancashire and Joseph Beasley of Northants.

Lancashire had been the prime movers in advocating that county matches should be restricted to two days in 1919. They feared that the war had reduced people's appetite for cricket, but they were proved wrong. The experiment of two-day county matches was a dreadful failure, and, thankfully, lasted only one season. One wishes the four-day game a similar life-span!

A.H. Hornby, 42 years old, had resigned as captain. He was replaced by the 33-year-old Kenyon. Kenyon was to become President of the County Club in 1936 and 1937 and was to be High Sheriff and Deputy Lieutenant of Lancashire, but when he stepped out as captain of the Lancashire cricket team on 19 May 1919, it was the first occasion on which he had ever appeared in first-class cricket. In fact, he scored 15, which was better than his average for the season, and even *Wisden*, ever tactful and deferential, found it hard to disguise some concern: 'The new captain, Mr M.N. Kenyon, though he lacked nothing in zeal, could not manage to make runs, first-class bowling being as yet a little too much for him. Moreover, he was unlucky in breaking down twice before the season ended.'

Kenyon averaged 14.70 during his career, and *Wisden*, in his obituary, drew attention to the innings of 24 he had played against the 1921 Australian side. He had under his command men of the calibre of E. and J.T. Tyldesley, Hallows and Makepeace. Parkin, one of the leading bowlers in England, played regularly after 1919. The quality of these players shadows any assessment that one can make on Kenyon's effect on the side as captain. They finished fifth three times and runners-up once during his period of leadership. His successor, Sharp, a far better player and one who had been a professional until 1919, had a very similar record, and it was not until Leonard Green took over that Lancashire won the title. But by then MacDonald, the Australian fast bowler, was in the side.

Green's record is remarkable. He was nowhere near as good a cricketer as John Sharp, who played three times for England in 1909, but he was an adequate batsman. He had a strength of character and a charming tact that was able to bring the best out of those under him. He turned a side of talented individuals into a winning team, and in his three years as captain, he led Lancashire to the title each season. No other captain in the history of the game can boast such an achievement, but few have had such an insight into the characters of others. Eventually he left the game because of the demands of business.

Whether or not the Lancashire committee had recognised outstanding leadership qualities in Green we know not. It is doubtful, for the general practice of counties at the time was simply to appoint an amateur of some stature (Green had been a Lieutenant-Colonel in the army) who was more or less regularly available.

In 1919, Northamptonshire had appointed Joseph Beasley as captain. They had been hard hit in that their pre-war skipper, S.G. Smith, a fine all-rounder, had not returned from the West Indies where he was born, but had, in fact, decided to settle in New Zealand. They turned to Beasley who had played three matches in 1911 in which he had scored 36 runs and taken two wickets. He had then emigrated to Australia, but returned to serve in the First World War in which he won the Military Cross. His year as captain of Northants went unmentioned in *Wisden*, and he left the game after 1919 to concentrate on farming. He carried with him a batting average of 6.25 and five first-class wickets which cost 52.20 runs each.

He was succeeded, in turn, by Raven, Tyler, Bull and Fitzroy, none of whom was a bowler, and whose career batting averages were 13.67, 14.19, 10.15 and 14.45 respectively. Quite simply, there were not enough amateurs of top quality available to lead county sides, yet figures should not be the only judgment on these men. G.M. Buckston, for example, averaged only 11.83 in his career, but he led Derbyshire through a very difficult period, and he and his family did much to help the County survive and prosper, and the same could be said of Whittington at Glamorgan and P.F.C. Williams at Gloucestershire, but it cannot be denied that the tradition and social demand that a first-class side must be led by an amateur put a severe strain on several counties, not least in weakening them in the field.

The Golden Age had its postscript with Pelham Warner leading Middlesex to the Championship in 1920. Now in the position of grand old man, and destined to be very powerful and influential in the game for the rest of his long life, Warner saw his side win their last nine matches and defeat Surrey in a dramatic manner on the last day of the season to take the title. Warner had been one of the selectors who had helped shape the side to go to Australia, 1920–21. He was, in fact, not on the selection committee, but had been asked to attend the final meeting in an advisory capacity.

The man invited to lead the side was R.H. Spooner who was 40 years old and played only six matches for Lancashire in 1920. He at first accepted and then, as he had done in the past, he declined the invitation. J.W.H.T. Douglas, two years junior to Spooner and already named in the party, was invited to captain in his place. The MCC had been reluctant to undertake the tour, and their task was not made easier by the inability of many of the leading amateurs to make the trip. D.J. Knight, G.E.C. Wood and V.W.C. Jupp all declined. P.G.H. Fender and Douglas were the only amateurs left from the original selection, and E.R. Wilson was added to boost the amateur contingent.

Percy Fender was not yet captain of Surrey and was never to be captain of England although he had his champions, and many considered him to be the best captain of the inter-war years. He was a fine all-rounder, a leg-spinner and ferociously hard-hitting batsman. He certainly did well with Surrey and was a splendid cricketer, and the argument had been forwarded that he was not named as England's captain because he was Jewish. Certainly there was a quietly effective anti-semitism at the time which would bar access to several clubs and golf clubs, but there were those in high places, Lord Harris among them, who may have considered Fender a little too adventurous as a leader and a little too arrogant as a man. *The Times*, on the other hand, considered Douglas too conservative:

> Colonel Douglas's abilities as a captain – like his ability as a player – are self-made and sound rather than brilliant. Perhaps his chief fault is lack of imagination, and an inability to realise that few men are possessed of his own inexhaustible stamina and keenness. But he is sufficiently shrewd, and very much a man.

In fact, Douglas gave hint of those qualities with which Armstrong and his Australians were to reshape Test cricket, a professional approach to the game and a ruthless dedication, but no captain in England could have halted the Australian advance. The Australians won the series by five Tests to nil, the first time such a whitewash had been achieved. Historians have spoken since of Douglas's over-reliance on pace, his belief that things would be as they had been nine years earlier and his general lack of ideas, but, in truth, the tools at his disposal were inadequate. The bowling was woefully weak. There was not a professional in the side who had a bad word to say against him, and one does not doubt that they gave their best, but often that is not good enough.

In England, the news of the defeats was received with disbelief; but when the Australians were seen in England a few months later their strength was recognised. The England cause was not helped by some bewildering work on the part of the selectors, R.H. Spooner, H.K. Foster and J. Daniell, who chose 30 players in the five Test matches of 1921.

Australia won the first Test by ten wickets, the second by eight wickets. Douglas had captained England in seven successive losing Tests. Like Gower 65 years later, he had to pay the price. The most common judgment on captains is that they are good if they win, bad if they lose. Douglas's eight Test wins were, like Gower's victories over Border's Australians, history; his seven defeats were current news. The selectors blindly sought to rekindle the spirit of the Golden Age. They failed to see, as only we see with the benefit of historical perspective, that Armstrong had moved cricket into a post-war era of ruthless efficiency and tactical expertise. He had brought a new dimension to field-placing and to probing at a batsman's weakness, crowding, frustrating and attacking with relentless power.

Douglas was lost against such a man, however dedicated his application. There was a belief that a re-establishment of the pre-war values would restore the balance. C.B. Fry, the epitome of all that was good and amateur, the man who could turn his hand to anything, would stem the flood. He had been asked to play in the Lord's Test, but he had withdrawn at the last moment because he felt he was not fit enough – he was 50 – and then he had been down to captain MCC against the Australians, but he had withdrawn from that match, too.

Nevertheless, Fry remained in the forefront of the action. He had told the selectors that Lionel Tennyson should play in the Lord's Test, and they obeyed him. He then agreed to captain England in the third Test at Leeds although Douglas was to remain in the side, but he damaged a finger when playing for Hampshire against the Australians on the eve of the Test and again withdrew. He remained as king-maker, however, and told the selectors that they should name Tennyson as captain. They did.

The irony of the Leeds Test was that Tennyson split a hand, and Douglas had to take over for a time. England lost, but Tennyson provided the colourful heroics for which there was a thirst. Batting one-handed against the fire and pace of MacDonald and Gregory, he scored 64 and 36. It was the type of glorious gesture for which the amateurs of the Golden Age had been renowned.

Grandson of the great Victorian poet, Lionel Hallam Tennyson, who became the third Baron Tennyson in 1928, did not play Test cricket after that 1921 series, the last two Tests of which were marred by rain and drawn, but he captained Hampshire until 1933. If one

Eccentric aristocrat – Lionel Tennyson.

man encapsulates the ideal of the amateur captain, it is Lord Tennyson. Hampshire never finished higher than sixth in the Championship under his leadership, and were generally considerably further down the table, and although he was a violent hitter of the ball and scored 19 first-class hundreds, he was totally unreliable and finished with a career average of just over 23. He infused his Hampshire side with the same trait of unpredictability, and if he led his side with limited tactical knowledge, he approached the game with an infectious aristocratic zest.

It would be wrong to say that he was a relic from the Golden Age. He was, as John Arlott so aptly put it, 'a misplaced Regency buck'. He lived life at a furious pace with a spectacular delight in all its pleasures. He played hard and for fun without a suggestion of a *professional* approach. Tactical subtlety was something beyond his comprehension, nor did he wish to comprehend it. He acted on impulse, and the impulses could as often bring defeat as victory.

'He was autocratic in a way which professional cricketers rarely can bring themselves to relish in their captain', wrote Arlott, 'and from which the amateur players under him were not immune. His decisions were usually hasty; he could be generous, but also, at times, quite insensitive to the feelings of others. At the prompting of a whim, he would all but reverse the side's batting order.'

'Yet,' Arlott continues while assessing the size and generosity of the man's character, 'it must be said that a captain of less playing ability, but with more tactical acumen, and above all, with greater tact in his dealings with men – especially professional cricketers – might have led the players available to the county in the early twenties to greater heights than ever were attained.'

Hampshire under Tennyson were at their most bizarre in June 1922, when they met Warwickshire at Edgbaston. Warwickshire batted first and made 223. Hampshire began their innings at four o'clock and were all out inside 45 minutes on a good wicket for 15, which included four byes. At the end of the innings, Tennyson shouted out 'Never mind, lads, we'll get 500 next time.' He then went round putting on bets, one of his favourite pastimes, that Hampshire would save the game. They did. They made 521, and then bowled Warwickshire out for 158 to win by 155 runs.

One of the Hampshire heroes was Walter Livesey, a fine wicket-keeper, who, batting at number ten, made a century. Livesey doubled in the role of Hampshire wicket-keeper and Tennyson's valet so that he rarely had a moment free from the demands of his employer/captain. One of the apocryphal stories surrounding the relationship concerns an appeal against the light which was rejected when master and servant were batting together. Tennyson called down the wicket that he wanted Livesey to watch him closely so that they could look for singles. Livesey shouted back, 'I'm afraid I can hear you, my Lord, but I can't see you.' The appeal against the light was upheld a few moments later.

It would seem incredible that Tennyson, with his limited knowledge of the game and temperamental uncertainty, should have the power to control the working lives of cricketers like Mead, Kennedy,

Brown and Boyes, Hampshire stalwarts of the time. It seems even more remarkable today to realise that when, in 1933, his last season, Tennyson missed several matches the Hampshire captaincy should be shared among whichever amateurs were available at the time. This meant that seven men led the County during the season, Brown and Mead among them when no amateurs were playing.

Rev. G.L.O. Jessop, son of the famous Gilbert 'The Croucher', made his first appearance for Hampshire against the West Indian tourists in May 1933. He had played one first-class match before this, for MCC four years earlier. He played his first match in the county championship, against Sussex at Horsham a month after the game with the West Indians.

The Hampshire side in the match at Horsham was Brown, Arnold, Bailey, Mead, Kennedy, Pothecary, Creese, Jessop, McCorkell, Boyes and Herman. McCorkell had made his debut the previous season. The rest had been in the side for at least four years. Mead had been playing for Hampshire since 1905. The side had 30 Test caps between them, and were to amass 4,477 appearances in first-class cricket. Bailey's 242 matches were to make him the least experienced member of the side. Yet the captain for the game at Horsham was Rev. G.L.O. Jessop, playing in his third first-class match, his first in the county championship. One more appearance, against Middlesex a week later, marked the end of his first-class career.

If it appears now that the tradition of having an amateur captain was taken to absurdity, it was, for the most part, a tradition that was accepted with little complaint. There was a legend that any time Derbyshire, Notts or Leicestershire needed a fast bowler, they simply went to the nearest coal pit and shouted down for one to come up. The life of a professional cricketer in the years between the wars had more to offer than work in a privately owned coal industry, with its poor conditions and bad wages, even if it did mean being led by somebody who knew less about the game than you did.

If the amateur owed his position of leadership to his class and education, he was bolstered, too, by the mystique with which these advantages were surrounded. University was a far more remote institution than it is today, so was the City, and there was an acceptance that the gentleman had a greater understanding of the mysteries and complexities of life than the player. On the cricket field, often aided by his colourful cap, he created a sense of all that was carefree, chivalrous and romantic. In effect, he made many believe that he was what they wished to be, untouched and untroubled by the drudgery of daily life.

That the amateur could transcend the sufferings of other mortals had been clearly demonstrated by A.C. MacLaren in 1921. While

England were being ravaged by Warwick Armstrong's Australians Archie MacLaren, nearing his 50th birthday, asserted that he could put a side in the field that would beat these intruders. His chance came at Easbourne on 27, 29 and 30 August when he chose and led An England XI composed entirely of amateurs. It was the 34th match of the Australian tour, and the visitors had won 20 and drawn 14 of their previous fixtures. They had already taken the Test series with three wins and two draws, and all that remained to them was a spree on the South Coast of which this match was a part and a festival game at Scarborough.

MacLaren's boast seemed a vain one when, on winning the toss, he chose to bat first on a perfect wicket and saw his side bowled out for 43 in 65 minutes. The Australians did not fare too well against Falcon and Faulkner, but they still took a first innings lead of 131. At 60 for 4 in their second innings, MacLaren's side looked well beaten, but Aubrey Faulkner, a South African, and Hubert Ashton batted magnificently to add 154. Faulkner went on to score 153, and the Australians were left to make 196. This did not seem a task which should worry the tourists, but Gibson, Falcon and Faulkner bowled with such control and aggression as to bring the England XI victory by 28 runs.

One feels that if the same result were achieved today – if, for example, a West Indian side which had walloped England in the Texaco Trophy and Cornhill Test matches were beaten in a festival match at Hastings or Scarborough – there would be only muted enthusiasm. In 1921, however, MacLaren's amateur eleven's victory over a tired Australian side who also lost the last match of their tour ten days later was the sensation of the season. It convinced people that the Golden Age lived on and that English cricket would prosper in the hands of the true amateur spirit.

The match was seen by few people and, as far as one can gather, by only one journalist, Neville Cardus of the *Manchester Guardian*. For Cardus, the match was a scoop and a scoop to which his poetic sensibilities responded. The memory of the match pervaded much of his writing for the next 50 years, and he implanted it in cricket history as one of the great events of the age. There was a ring of Agincourt about it.

It had all the right ingredients. The all amateur side had heroes like Falcon and Gibson whose appearances in first-class cricket were restricted to a handful of matches. Percy Chapman and Hubert Ashton were young university men who breathed the hope of the future. Walter Brearley was a rebellious spirit from the past and 45 years old, his first-class career nearly a decade behind him. The side had been bowled out for 43 on the first morning, but had risen like the phoenix to claim victory. And then there was MacLaren.

It is likely that the boast and the subsequent victory in this match have coloured opinions as to MacLaren's true worth as a captain. There can be no doubt that he was a fine batsman, but his record as a captain is a poor one.

He was popular in Australia, as are most losing England captains, and went there in 1894–5, 1897–8 and 1901–02. He was captain of the side on his last tour and for much of his second tour when Stoddart was indisposed. As we have noted, he was indirectly responsible for Grace's Test career coming to an end, being brought in for the second Test at Lord's and assuming the captaincy. He lost the series as he did all other series in which he was captain, and, in fact, he captained England in 22 Tests against Australia and won only four of them while he lost eleven.

He captained Lancashire from 1900 to 1907, and they won the Championship in 1904 and were nearly always in contention, but he left the uneasy feeling that the side would have done better under somebody else. He had a fine strategic grasp, but he was imperious in mien, too authoritarian. His failings in the important sphere of man management had disastrous effects. H.S. Altham, a perceptive and balanced historian, felt that MacLaren 'rather lacked the gift of making others believe in, and so make the best of, themselves.'

The inescapable fact is that MacLaren was a bad captain, yet such was the magnetic power of the man's eccentric personality that many close to him felt that there had been none better. R.H. Spooner was of this opinion and wrote so in *The Times* when MacLaren died. One of his values was that he was more available to tour Australia than men like Spooner himself or Fry although his financial basis always seemed to be an uncertain one.

Douglas's record as a captain in the years before the First World War is far better than MacLaren's, and Douglas carried on his back a weak and unfashionable county, but MacLaren was surrounded with a glamour which Douglas was not. The glamour lasted beyond his playing days. He mellowed with age, perhaps, and was coach at Old Trafford for a couple of seasons. He also took an MCC side to Australia and New Zealand in 1922–23 and hit a double century in a 'Test' against New Zealand, but one wonders what his reputation would be had he not led his side to victory over the Australians at Eastbourne.

The finest cricket reference book of the past ten years or so, *Who's Who of Cricketers*, so correct in all else, is seduced by him. He is 'regarded by some contemporaries as England's best captain. Everyone is agreed that he was a great tactical expert, but whilst he led his country he was criticised for his part in the selection of some of the England teams. At the end of his career, however, he silenced his critics by choosing a side to meet the strong 1921 Australian team and, against all odds, beating them when everyone else had failed.'

Never can one match have had such a total influence on people's later thinking. The *Manchester Guardian* touched the right chord in the obituary of MacLaren which they published in 1944 when they said that his cricket 'belonged to the golden age of the game, to the spacious and opulent England of his day; it knew not the common touch.'

The victory at Eastbourne, and the perpetuation of its memory, convinced people that 'the spacious and opulent England' could be reborn. The only difficulty was to find the right leader, the man who could open the door to the past.

Tennyson evoked dreams, but his weaknesses as a captain and as a player were manifest. Frank Mann led Middlesex and England with panache, but business claimed him, and then Arthur Gilligan glimmered briefly to suggest that he would lead English cricket out of the wilderness.

Arthur Gilligan's career was frustrated by the war, but his quick bowling impressed at Cambridge in 1919 and after a few games for Surrey he joined Sussex, captaining them from 1922 to 1929. He did not transform them into a title-winning side, but he brought a breath of fresh air to the South Coast with his emphasis on good fielding and a positive approach to the game. He could bat with zest, and his bowling combination with Maurice Tate became formidable for Sussex and England.

Gilligan was genuinely quick, and when he was chosen to captain England against South Africa in 1924 it could be argued that he had been picked as a player as much as a leader, for he would certainly have earned a place in the side on merit for his bowling alone which he quickly proved by taking 6 for 7 as South Africa were bowled out for 30. A few weeks earlier, he and Tate had bowled out Surrey for 53 and Middlesex for 41 so that there was nothing totally abnormal in their rout of South Africa.

It seemed that England had found the lost leader, and hopes were high for the tour to Australia the following winter. By the end of June, Gilligan had taken 74 wickets at low cost. The previous year he had done the 'double', and there was excitement in the air, but disaster was looming. Playing for the Gentlemen against the Players at The Oval in July, he was struck over the heart when batting. The injury was serious, but he insisted on playing on, and he hit 112 in 90 minutes in the second innings. It was brave, but foolhardy. He undoubtedly worsened the injury, and although he was to play for another eight years, he was never the same bowler again. He was never able to bowl really quickly again, and he subsided to being little more than a change bowler.

He led England to Australia in 1924–5, and Tate bowled heroically while Sutcliffe batted magnificently. A Test match was won, but four were lost. From that point, Gilligan's career slipped quietly to its close although he was to serve the game nobly in various capacities for another 50 years.

5 The Age of Bradman

Gilligan's decline again left England leaderless with the Australians arriving in 1926, victorious in three consecutive series since the war. Green was just beginning his triumphant reign at Old Trafford, but could not be considered a Test cricketer. Frank Mann could give less and less time to the game. Daniell, Calthorpe and Cornwallis were admirable men, but hardly up to confronting the Australians. J.C. Clay of Glamorgan was yet to prove himself, and Fender, though the choice of many, was not to be favoured by the selectors.

Gilligan's vice-captain in Australia had been Johnny Douglas, but he was 44 years old, past his best and no longer a serious contender. The rest of the county captains were scarcely of first-class standard. The only possible man for the job was A.W. Carr.

Arthur Carr had been unable to hold a regular place in the Notts side until he became captain in 1919. Like Douglas, Carr made himself into a good cricketer. He became a consistently successful hard-hitting batsman and a fine fielder. He lived hard and played tough, and under him, Notts were a formidable side, always challenging for the title and winning it in 1929 when they brought a temporary end to Lancashire's monopoly.

Carr was forthright and outspoken. He was a public-school man, excelled at many sports and accepted leadership as the position to which he had been born. He did, however, represent the new attitude towards captaincy and games at which Douglas had hinted and which was to find its fruition in Jardine. Carr was the professional amateur, aware of a changing world. He was not one to look over his shoulder wistfully at the sunlit age of the Edwardians.

Certainly the world was changing, although the fermentation of unrest which brought the General Strike at the beginning of May

Arthur Carr.

1926, and 'brought the country nearer to revolution than it has ever been', was to abate and flounder into the political stagnation and despair of the hungry thirties. One significant change in cricket was that the selection committee, Warner, Perrin and Arthur Gilligan, was instructed to co-opt two professionals, one from the north and one from the south, who would have the same powers as the rest of the committee. This may seem a slight matter today, but one must remember that not until Leslie Ames was named as a Test selector in 1950 was a professional ever accorded that status. In 1926, the co-opted members were Jack Hobbs and Wilfred Rhodes.

Arthur Carr was named as captain and joined the committee to choose the side. His appointment was generally welcomed. The non-appointment of Fender was more accepted at the time than it has been since. Carr was uncompromising and, at times, controversial, but he was seen as the man tough enough to deal with the Australians. The country was thirsting for success.

The first Test was ruined by rain, the second was drawn. The England bowling had not been strong, but the batting had given them the upper hand. Warner combined the duties of chairman of selectors, editor of *The Cricketer* and cricket correspondent of the *Morning Post*. The licence that was accorded to the man is still staggering to consider. No ex-professionnal would have been granted such freedom which could be interpreted as a conflict of interests. After the second Test, Warner was in ecstasies about Carr whom he saw as inspiring, 'absorbed in his job' and 'the best captain England has had for many a long day'.

A captain is always good when things are going well. Carr's popularity was short-lived, at least as far as the chairman of selectors was concerned. In the third Test, he won the toss, asked Australia to bat first and saw them get 494. Carr himself dropped Macartney off the fifth ball of the match after Bardsley had been caught at slip off the first. Macartney went on to make 151. The general feeling was that the missed chance haunted Carr and affected his captaincy which, if it did, would suggest a temperamental weakness. England were asked to follow-on, but they were saved by Hobbs and Sutcliffe.

There were rumblings that a mistake had been made in omitting Charlie Parker of Gloucestershire, the most successful spin bowler in the country, and that Carr was to blame. Another faction held that Carr wanted Parker in the side but was forced to play Macaulay. Parker was also omitted from the side for the fourth Test. He was to miss selection for every Test during the span of his career, except for one in 1921. As he took 3,278 wickets and was, at times, unplayable, it is hard to comprehend, except that recent research has revealed that he was not a favourite of Warner's.

The fourth Test match was also drawn. Rain disrupted play on the Saturday, and there was never any likelihood of a result. During the match Carr developed tonsillitis. The only other amateur in the side was Greville Stevens, the Middlesex all-rounder, but he had played so little cricket and was so lacking in experience even though he was 25 that it was not felt wise that he should take over. Jack Hobbs led the side in Carr's absence. He was the best batsman in the world and a thoughtful and dignified man. His handling of the England side in Carr's absence was described as masterly, but, as he was a professional, there was no question of him taking over on a regular basis.

The fifth Test was to be played to a finish as the four previous Tests had been drawn. Carr arrived late at the selection meeting on 8 August, rather as Fry had done a quarter of a century before. He knew instinctively when he arrived that something was wrong. He was to be sacked. The official reason given was that he was still unwell, although Carr refuted this. He insisted that he was eager, fit and willing to play, but to save embarrassment, he withdrew from the meeting. Warner's part in the proceedings once more do not reflect well on the man.

The two sensational changes that the selectors made were to recall Wilfred Rhodes to Test cricket within a few weeks of his 50th birthday and to appoint Percy Chapman as captain. Chapman had been left out of the side for the fourth Test and had not been born when Rhodes first played for England.

There was outrage at the dismissal of Carr, but Warner, naturally, was behind Chapman. 'Was not Pitt Prime Minister at 25, and does not Pembroke, Cambridge, claim both Pitt and Chapman?'

England won a famous victory, and Chapman was received as a national hero. He had led English cricket out of the wilderness, and the Ashes were back where they belonged.

Chapman was, in many ways, an anachronism. A schoolboy prodigy at Uppingham, he had excited the cricket world at Cambridge with his free, left-handed batting, his wonderfully athletic fielding and the looks of a Greek god. Here, surely, was the Golden Age reincarnated. He hit a sparkling hundred in the Varsity match at Lord's and for the Gentlemen against the Players at Lord's. He had toured Australia and New Zealand with MacLaren's side and Australia with Gilligan's side. What is more he had been in MacLaren's side which had beaten the Australians at Eastbourne in 1921.

He was socially acceptable, warm, friendly and hospitable. He was liked by all. Unfortunately, he had not had too much experience of first-class cricket outside university. He was born in Berkshire and was a minor-county cricketer when he first appeared for England. He qualified for Kent by residence, and at the beginning of the 1926 season in which he was to lead England for the first time, his record stood as follows:

Percy Chapman and his wife on the day that Chapman was named as captain of England, August 1926.

Six Test matches, 193 runs, average 27.57
Five games for Kent, 213 runs, average 23.66

His experience of captaincy was even more limited, and he was not to be elected captain of Kent until 1931, by which time his career was already in decline; yet the fact that he was captain of England when they regained the Ashes at The Oval in 1926 leaves him revered in the minds of many today. Perhaps we should examine the part he played in that victory.

Chapman won the toss and chose to bat. At lunch, England were 108 for 3, and Chapman came out after lunch to bat with Sutcliffe who was unbeaten on 40. Warner wrote of Chapman, 'He had a captain's job to do, and he was intent on doing it. His men stood in need of moral as well as material succour, and it was his duty and privilege to supply both.' But Chapman was an instinctive player, a hitter. This was the characteristic which made him so immensely popular, for followers remember only a hitter's successes and forget the failures. When he had first been chosen for England there were those who felt, with some justification, that his technique would prove insufficient at Test level.

His response to the situation at The Oval on the first afternoon of his first match as captain of England was to play his natural game. He hit 49 out of a stand of 81 with Sutcliffe and was out, stumped, when he charged down the wicket in an attempt to hit Mailey out of the ground and missed. More than half a century later Ian Botham was castigated when, having brought England to the point of victory in a Texaco Trophy match, he was out playing a reverse sweep, but in 1926, Chapman's swashbuckling miniature innings on the first afternoon of a timeless Test was generally accepted as being just what was wanted.

Disappointingly, England were all out by five o'clock, but Australia, a much weaker side than they had been in 1921 and in 1924–5, were 60 for 4 by the close. They still took a first innings lead of 22, and the match was in the balance with Hobbs and Sutcliffe together at the end of the second day.

A violent storm broke over London that evening, and The Oval was saturated, but the wicket had dried out enough for play to begin at eleven the next morning. Hobbs and Sutcliffe faced the stiffest of tasks, facing Grimmett and Mailey on a wicket which gave them every assistance. In one of the greatest batting displays Test cricket has known, they put on 172 for England's first wicket; Hobbs made 100 and Sutcliffe 161. Could any captain really have influenced them in what they did? There were failings on the part of the Australians which aided them, but what of Chapman? Hobbs and Sutcliffe were blended into the greatest opening partnership England has had, and by 1926 they were at the height of their powers. They would have battled to survive and win on a sticky wicket whoever the captain.

England made 436, and then bowled and caught in a manner which mocked the Australian effort. Chapman may have been inspirational in this respect, but England had their tails up and fortune was smiling on them. Rhodes had taken four wickets and Larwood three, but Chapman took them both off to give Stevens and Geary a chance to take a wicket and share in the glory. It was hardly a sign of tactical genius, and it was certainly a frivolity of which Rhodes did not approve, but England won, and on the strength of that victory the likeable Chapman was hailed both as a good captain and as a young man of genius.

Working in the brewery trade, a fact which was to cause much of the sadness and pain of his later years, Chapman was not always readily available for first-class cricket. He could not tour South Africa and when West Indies came to England in 1928 the name of Douglas Jardine was being forwarded as the greatest amateur batsman the country had known since R.H. Spooner, but Chapman quickly reasserted himself. There was, perhaps, an unspoken unease that he was not quite so fit as he had been, and there was a tendency to put on weight, but he had the capacity to make people happy. He was kind, generous, cheery and encouraging. He was among the most popular public figures in England. He led England to victory in all three Tests against the West Indies and was named as captain for the team to tour Australia.

It was a side immensely strong in batting. Wally Hammond had just come into his prime and was to dominate a series in which every match was played to a finish. Australia, on the other hand, were in a transitional period. It was a series in which Bradman was to make his début but was not to establish himself.

With Chapman as captain, England won the first four Test matches, the first two by huge margins. He stood down from the last Test because of injury and England lost. Players loved him. The crowd loved him. There was magic in the man – or so some believed. At a time when there was mass unemployment and economic depression he was a beacon of hope – eight matches as England's captain, eight victories.

Returning late to England after a holiday in New Zealand and suffering injury when playing for Kent against Sussex, Chapman's appearances in the 1929 season were limited. J.C. White and A.W. Carr led England in the series against South Africa which England won. These were heady days for talent, and in 1929–30, England sent touring teams to both New Zealand and West Indies; but the only series that really mattered in the period between the wars were those which saw England and Australia in opposition.

The Australians arrived in 1930 with England in buoyant mood. Chapman had played little and had put on weight, but there was a clamour that he should lead the side. More sober commentators stated quite plainly that he was no longer good enough, nor fit enough, but he hit a century for Kent against Somerset, had a great success as captain of MCC against the Australians at Lord's and eventually was named to captain England in the first Test.

Not all were convinced about this appointment. It was believed that Carr was out of the running for political reasons, and that Duleepsinhji, a brilliant batsman and soon to be a highly successful captain of Sussex, was not considered for reasons of colour. He was certainly left out of the side against South Africa the previous season for that reason.

All criticism was silenced, however, when Chapman, batting

excitingly, catching splendidly and leading quite memorably on the last day when he was without Larwood, led England to victory over Australia in the first Test at Trent Bridge by 93 runs. This was Chapman's sixth victory in succession over Australia, a feat which remains unequalled. Bradman had hit a century, but England had won. Chapman was again a national hero.

He remained a national hero even though he lost a Test match for the first time when Australia, with Bradman making 254 in under five and a half hours, won at Lord's. In the second innings, Chapman, with his side facing defeat, hit 121 in 155 minutes. His innings included four sixes and twelve fours, and it gave him a record that will never be equalled, a century in the Varsity match, the Gentleman and Players match and a Test match at Lord's.

In spite of Chapman's gloriously brave innings, Australia needed only 72 to win, a formality, but even so Chapman took a stunning catch in the gulley to send back Bradman, and, in defeat, Chapman was acclaimed as enthusiastically as he had been in victory. He was responsible for England's enthusiasm, and the press believed that he had implanted himself permanently in the Test side. Yet A.A. Milne, better known for Pooh than for cricket, wrote a comment that was revealing of the changing attitudes of the time. 'These days of over-professionalism, when captains are rather lucky to be playing at all, they go in sixth, after the rungetters are out, and show them how cricket ought to be played. Chapman did this as bravely as I have ever seen it done.'

The sentiment is rather questionable. Certainly some captains were lucky to be playing in sides for which they were not good enough, but many of them were not capable of showing 'how cricket ought to be played'. As to Chapman's worth at Test level, several still nursed doubts in their hearts.

Chapman was not helped by his selection committee who made five changes after England's defeat at Lord's, leaving out Robins and Woolley who had been the most impressive bowler and batsman, respectively, in the second test.

The third and fourth Tests were drawn. Before the fourth Test, which was ruined by rain, Chapman had accepted the invitation to lead England in South Africa, but, even as, wearing his Quidnunc cap, he walked on to the field at Old Trafford, there were moves behind the scenes to replace him as captain for the fifth and final Test. Warner knew of the conspiracy and was part of it. The press knew of it, and some started a campaign to stop it. They were not successful.

The selectors themselves, with Hobbs and Rhodes again co-opted, appeared to be in disarray. R.E.S. Wyatt was brought in as captain, fourteen players, including two wicket-keepers, were chosen, and

Parker, so long in the wilderness, was recalled at the age of 46 and then left out of the side on the morning of the match.

The selectors were roundly condemned, as was the unfortunate Wyatt, a solid and capable batsman never popular as captain. The nation rallied behind Chapman. The debate was intense and at times unpleasant. At The Oval, Australia, batting second, scored 695 and won by an innings. There was sadness for England, anger at the selectors.

To win nine Test matches in succession and to be dropped when you first lose one has not been the lot of any other captain, but Milne's passage gives a hint as to the reason. Chapman had performed nobly in the Tests, but doubts as to his quality at international level remained, particularly in what was to be a timeless Test. As a captain he was much liked for his cheeriness, his friendliness and his inspirational qualities, but he was not a great thinker, on or off the field. He did not possess the tactical knowledge or ability to cope with Bradman. His Kent side would say of him in the few remaining years of his career that he would stand immovable at silly point whatever the state of the game. He played his cricket in a Golden Age of his own imagination. Life never ceased to be August 1926 for him, and cricket's increased professional resolution, the 'over-professionalism', went by unnoticed.

It was clearly noticed by others, particularly by those in the north. Between the wars the story of Yorkshire was one of almost uninterrupted success, twelve titles and only once, 1934, as low as fifth in the Championship. If the south seemed anxious to preserve an amateur spirit, which could be interpreted as a social enjoyment of the game without worrying too much about the result, the northern counties were concerned about winning and adopted an attitude which would bring this about. Between 1922 and 1946, only four counties won the Championship, and they were the northern counties: Yorkshire, Lancashire, Nottinghamshire and Derbyshire. Yorkshire dominance and professionalism did not endear the county to many of the southern gentry.

The Yorkshire side was forceful in character, and the support that they engendered was fanatical. In May 1924, having not been beaten in the Championship for over a year, Yorkshire came to Lord's without Holmes, Sutcliffe, Kilner and Macaulay, who were playing in a Test trial, as were the Middlesex pair, Hendren and Hearne. A predominantly amateur Middlesex eleven won by an innings, and the Yorkshire reaction was tantamount to avowing that this defeat must be avenged as soon as possible.

The return match was at Sheffield in July. The game began in an atmosphere of ill-will. Yorkshire won the toss and asked Middlesex to

R.E.S. Wyatt. Never fortunate as England's captain.

bat first on a soft wicket. Middlesex survived, and the game was drawn. Used to success, some of the Yorkshire players behaved petulantly when they were frustrated in their desire to win. Bowlers incited partisan spectators with a succession of appeals. The umpires were put under severe pressure, and the game grew more unpleasant as it progressed.

The umpires, Butt and Reeves, reported the conduct of the match to MCC and named the Yorkshire bowler Waddington as the main culprit. Middlesex left Sheffield vowing that they would not meet Yorkshire in future seasons. An enquiry suggested that the Yorkshire players should keep their feelings under control while negotiations between the two counties ended with Middlesex agreeing to play Yorkshire in 1925.

The lack of discipline and control in the Yorkshire side did not reflect well on their captain Geoffrey Wilson, a Harrovian and Cambridge blue of limited ability. He was a member of MacLaren's side that toured Australia and New Zealand in 1922–3, and in his three years as captain of Yorkshire, he led the side to three successive Championships. The part that he played in these successes is hard to assess. He led a side of immense talent which, fired by a passion for their county, had a relentless desire to win. He was handicapped by an operation for appendicitis during his first season, and it is interesting to note that, whatever his contribution as captain, it has gone unrecorded by the several men who have written histories of the Club. His name is not mentioned in Sutcliffe's autobiography nor, more significantly, does Lord Hawke speak of him in his *Recollections and Reminiscences* which was published in 1924 when Wilson was the Yorkshire captain. One is tempted to think that the amateur captain of Yorkshire was almost an irrelevance, a sop to convention while the team got on and won without worrying too much about him.

As Yorkshire President, Lord Hawke had to work hard in the diplomatic circles of cricket to placate the southern attitude to his county's approach to the game. Wilson resigned as captain and was succeeded by Major Arthur Lupton.

Lupton had played once for Yorkshire in 1908. He was 46 years old, and he was most kindly referred to as an enthusiastic club cricketer. His main function was to concentrate his attention on the duties of discipline and public relations, allowing the players to get on with the cricket. He had no background knowledge of the game to fit him for the post of Yorkshire captain. He was appointed because of his station in life.

It is generally accepted that it was Wilfred Rhodes, rich in experience and understanding of the game, who made most of the decisions on the field. There is a tale that, on one occasion, Lupton was buckling on his pads preparatory to taking his place in the lower order when one of his men said to him, 'There's no hurry, Major, I think Wilfred's going to declare.'

In his first year as captain, Yorkshire won the title, and he led the side until the end of the 1927 season. Lancashire were now the dominant county, and Yorkshire had to look closely at their future prospects, particularly after the sudden death of Kilner and the retirement of Waddington. The departure of Lupton again raised the question of captaincy, for there was a distinct shortage of candidates for the post, at least if the prevalent convention was adhered to.

Sutcliffe wrote later of the difficulty in finding a captain who has the all-round equipment for the job. 'There are skippers who, while they have personality, lack skill, and there are those who have skill without personality. I don't know which of them is the better off, but I can say I have known moderate players with personality get on better than good players without personality.'

Wilson's 985 runs, average 12.31, and Lupton's 668 runs, average 10.27, must place them in the first category, for they won four titles between them as captains, and Lupton added a second place and a third place in his other two seasons.

The committee debated long and hard over the problem of Lupton's successor, and they became the first men to face up honestly to the reality of the situation when they announced that the captaincy of the county was to be offered to Herbert Sutcliffe and that he would remain a professional. The announcement caused immediate controversy, especially as it came from a county traditionally conservative in views and with a president who had made a famous remark concerning professionals captaining England at an AGM only two years earlier.

The decision could not have been an easy one for Yorkshire, and, initially, there had been a suggestion that Sutcliffe be asked to become an amateur and that he be recompensed by a testimonial and some form of employment outside the game to cover any financial loss. Thankfully, this hypocrisy was avoided.

The hostility that greeted the appointment was intense, and it came on two fronts: one, that Sutcliffe was a professional; two, that Rhodes was senior to him and should have been offered the job were a professional to be approached. As Rhodes was 50 years old, the last objection was silly, and no criticism could be levelled at Sutcliffe as a cricketer and as a man. He was England's opening batsman, impeccably dressed, well-mannered and well-liked. He had served as an officer in the Green Howards during the war.

When he was invited to become captain of Yorkshire, a unanimous decision by a committee who considered no other candidate, Sutcliffe

Herbert Sutcliffe turned down the offer of the Yorkshire captaincy because he was a professional.

was with the MCC side in South Africa, an England XI rather curiously captained by Captain R.T. Stanyworth who had yet to play county cricket, but who was to play three times for Yorkshire in 1928. Sutcliffe, not, one feels, without some pressure upon him, declined the invitation. 'Official invitation received yesterday. Many thanks to you and your committee for great honour. Have carefully considered question and regret to decline. Am willing to play under any captain elected.'

The establishment breathed a sigh of relief. Warner, in his editorial to the Spring Annual of *The Cricketer*, 1928, was much comforted by Sutcliffe's refusal. 'The question arose as to whether it would not be wise to have a professional. One was selected, and very wisely, in our opinion, declined to act. There is not a word to be said against the professional of today, but the position is such that it is difficult – more so than many think – for him to sit in judgment on his fellow players.'

The man to whom Yorkshire were forced to turn to sit in judgment was William, later Sir William, Worsley, father of the present Duchess of Kent. He had never before played first-class cricket, but it was predicted by those who were gratified that the accepted order remained intact that he would 'be able to strengthen Yorkshire's batting by contributing the dash and enterprise which are needed in the middle part of the order'. This was a claim that the likeable, but inexperienced, Worsley was hardly likely to justify, particularly as he usually batted at number ten and only once as high as eight in his two years with the side.

His successor, Alan Barber, was an Oxford blue from a Sheffield family of distinguished cricketers. In his season as captain of Yorkshire, he hit 792 runs, but it was his leadership rather than his batting which won approval. Sutcliffe said of him that he 'had method in every move he made, and had personality, he earned the respect and comradeship of every member of the side. A great captain was A.T. Barber – one of those rare men with the power of inspiring confidence.'

This was mighty praise, and there was genuine sadness when Barber stepped down after only a year because he had been offered an excellent post in the academic world. Frank Greenwood took over from Barber and led with enterprise as well as contributing consistently with the bat, but it was his successor, Brian Sellers, who was to bring about the total restoration of Yorkshire pride and to lead the county to a supremacy which only Surrey in the 1950s has equalled.

Like Douglas and Carr, Sellers did not believe that he was good enough as a player when he moved from the Bradford League to first-class cricket, and he resolved to work at his game. Few men have worked with more determination, but when, in the years just before the Second World War, he was forwarded by some as a possible captain of England, he maintained that he was not good enough as a player. At county level, however, his resolution would have earned him a place in the side on merit, and as a fielder he had no superior. J.M. Kilburn, a writer close to the Yorkshire eleven of Sellers' day, gives the best assessment of the man:

> The aspect of courage in his character gave him the desired and admired qualities of leadership. He was an inspiration through the longest day in the field. In the covers he was untiring and he developed a notable capacity to pick up and throw powerfully on the turn, sometimes with both feet off the ground. In the close positions of gully, silly mid-off or on the leg side he was always prepared to be a leader, never asking his players to take risks he was not prepared to accept for himself
>
> He was essentially of the team as distinct from being with the team. Their interests and their welfare were his and however scathing he might have had to be in private dressing-room discipline his public identification was always with his players. He represented them loyally in committee and he was their advocate in all matters beneficial to their comfort and efficiency.

The side that Sellers had at his command, of course, was one of exceptional talent, but he brought them to a self-discipline and unity which not all gifted teams have achieved.

While Sellers was establishing Yorkshire on a truly professional basis, in attitudes and approach on the field, and in treatment of players, others were not so far-sighted. In Kent, Brian Valentine and 'Hopper' Levett, fine amateur players, both received reprimands for familiarity with professionals in the use of christian names. Les Ames, the greatest wicket-keeper batsman the world has known, arrived for a match at Lord's with his wife and was asked for an entrance fee of 1s 6d for her. He refused to pay and they both entered the ground. Later in the day he was called into the office of the secretary of MCC, strongly reprimanded and forced to pay the entrance fee for his wife. Somerset became noted for omitting many of its professionals in late July and throughout August in order to accommodate the considerable band of amateur players who were on holiday.

The professionalism which Sellers had inculcated at Yorkshire was not to the liking of all, and the scars were still to be seen after the Second World War when Freddie Truman's overtures of friendliness were turned aside by some who felt that they had suffered at Yorkshire's hands in the 1930s and that the relentless pursuit of victory was not the way in which cricket should be played. There were some who felt this at international level.

The dismissal of Chapman brought about a significant change in English cricket at Test level, for those that followed him were men surer of their place in an international side by dint of their ability. They were amateurs because they were not paid for playing cricket, but they were not amateurs in the sense that MacLaren, Fry or

Brian Sellers led Yorkshire to dominance in the 1930s.

Chapman had been amateurs, dashing in style and eccentric in personality. Bob Wyatt was a determined batsman who hit nearly 40,000 runs in his career and averaged 31.70 in his 40 Tests. Douglas Jardine's Test average was 48, and he headed the first-class averages in 1927 and 1928 with 87.15 and 91.09 respectively.

Jardine had been in Chapman's side in Australia in 1928–29 and captained England in the home Tests against New Zealand and India in 1931 and 1932. As the man in power, captain of Surrey and without a blemish on his record as batsman or leader, Jardine would have appeared to be the automatic choice to take the side to Australia in 1932, but there were those in power who were far from happy to entrust the side to him. It was recognised that he had a strong desire to win, that he was not of the amateur spirit, but of professional resolution. Others were sounded out, among them Hubert Ashton who had been unable to play much first-class cricket since leaving university, but who, it will be remembered, played an important part in bringing victory to MacLaren's side over the Australians at Eastbourne in 1921. It is remarkable how long memories of that game echoed down the years as a reminder as to what the true amateur spirit could achieve against this new professionalism. It was Jardine, however, who took the side to Australia.

England won four of the five Test matches in a series which acquired the epithet 'bodyline'. Warner, one of the two managers of the party, seemed at first to support Jardine's tactics in bowling his fast men, Larwood and Voce, to a packed leg-side field, although he later recanted and said it was wrong ethically. Of Jardine, he wrote

> Jardine had many admirable qualities, and was as good a tactician as any captain I have ever seen. He planned and thought and never spared himself and set a fine example of physical fitness. He was absolutely unselfish and would never ask anyone to do anything which he would not do himself. Especially was he a master in the art of changing his bowling and in keeping his bowlers fresh.

Jardine went to Australia to recover the Ashes. He recognised that the biggest obstacle to his achieving success was Don Bradman, the greatest run-getter that the game has known. Jardine's plans were formulated to nullify Bradman, and they did, although in his 'failure' series, Bradman still averaged more than 50.

Jardine was tough and uncompromising in the way that Sellers was and Close would be. He was the logical development of Douglas and Carr although he was better equipped as a player than both and a much deeper and more objective thinker than Douglas. He was the professional amateur, totally dedicated to the idea of winning. Cricket was a serious business for Jardine, not, in spite of the Harlequin cap which he wore to antagonise the Australians, some frivolous exercise of which only the social intercourse, rather than the outcome of the match, was of importance.

Victorious, Jardine was badly supported by those who had chosen him, badly supported by a manager who was ever on the side of the angels. He was never let down by players, who had the greatest admiration for him.

Sutcliffe, almost unique among professionals in that he wrote his book *For Yorkshire and England* unaided by a 'ghost', called Jardine 'one of the greatest men I have met'. He recognised that Jardine lacked showmanship which would have made him more popular with crowds, that he was stern, and that his integrity was unwavering. 'Jardine had the courage of his convictions; it was unfortunate for him that they did not meet with general approval, but that did not alter his

Iron man Douglas Jardine, leader in the controversial bodyline tour.

outlook. He planned for us, he cared for us, he fought for us on that tour, and he was so faithful in everything he did that we were prepared on our part to do anything we could for him. A great cricket captain.'

But Jardine was sacrificed, as was Larwood, so that peace could be restored, and Bradman came to England in 1934 and pillaged more and more runs against an England side that was rudderless. When next England went to Australia, 1936–37, G.O. Allen, born in Australia, was in charge. It was a goodwill mission, and England, two up in the series, lost the last three Tests and peace was restored.

Allen led England in three Test series, the others being against India in 1936 and in the West Indies in 1947–48 when he was 45 years old. He was a good fast bowler and a very capable batsman, but in 29 years he played only 146 games for Middlesex and was never the county captain. His appointment to lead England in the West Indies in 1947 surprised many people, none more than Tom Pearce, the Essex captain, who had been approached by Warner to captain the side. He arranged leave of absence with the wine firm for whom he worked and then read in a newspaper that Allen was to take the side.

Any problems as to who should be captain of England in the late 1930s were solved when, after the 1937 season, Wally Hammond announced that he would, in future, play as an amateur. He had been England's leading batsman for a decade, and in world cricket only Bradman was his superior. That his initials were now written in front of his name instead of after meant that he was acceptable as England's captain although, as a man, he was no different from what he had always been. In fact, in character and personality he was far from ideal as a captain. He was a complex man, far too concerned for his own form as a batsman to be able to look at a match dispassionately or objectively. He was a glorious stroke-player and a highly entertaining batsman to watch, but too introverted, too much the victim of his own fallibilities.

Hammond represented the second stage in the crisis of captaincy. Whereas amateurs who were inadequate players had been chosen to lead sides because of their station in life, now there was a captain who was the best player on the side, but who had deficiencies when it came to qualities of leadership. Nevertheless, he led Gloucestershire to third place in the Championship in 1939, won series against South Africa and West Indies and drew with Bradman's 1938 Australians.

At county level, it was still not easy to find an amateur who could spare sufficient time for the game who could lead a side capably. When Douglas was finally forced to stand down as captain of Essex in 1928 he did so with bitterness. His argument was that the county had not found a suitable replacement for him. He was proved right in that his immediate successor, H.M. Morris, could never give the time to the game. In his last season as captain, he appeared only once. Tom Pearce was excellent, but he had to share the job with Denys Wilcox, a splendid batsman from Cambridge who might well have captained England had he not had to give so much time to his scholastic duties. In 1939, the Essex captaincy was shared between three players.

In the early 1930s Middlesex slumped badly until Walter Robins took over in 1935. He was the south's counterpart of Brian Sellers, having a dynamic will to win and a ruthless efficiency. He was a good leg-break bowler, an attacking batsman and a brilliant fielder. He drove people hard, and there was never any doubt as to who was captain of the side. Denis Compton is one of several who believes that Robins was the best captain he ever saw, but Compton admits that he was despotic and could ruin a young cricketer with the sharpness and damnation of his tongue. Even Dexter argued that it was remarks that Robins made to Barrington during the interval of the Old Trafford Test against Australia in 1961, that cost England the game, but, in defence of Robins, he was by then a sick man. He certainly caused some hackles to rise with his authoritarian attitude when he managed the MCC side in the West Indies, 1959–60, not realising, perhaps, that times were changing.

Glamorgan were most capably led until the outbreak of war by the quiet, determined and tactful Maurice Turnbull who was a batsman of distinction. Had he played for a more fashionable county, he might well have captained England, for he led one of the sides in a Test trial although his nine matches for England brought him only moderate success. He was killed in action in 1944 and one of his former colleagues, and another Glamorgan captain, J.C. Clay, said of him that he believed there had been no better captain. He was never fussy, nor given to shouting or gesticulating. He got the best out of a side of limited ability, and he had the capacity for making bowlers feel that 'although the scoreboard said otherwise, they were really doing pretty well'. He did much for the professionals whom he led, and they responded with devotion. His knowledge was recognised when he was made a Test selector.

Wyatt fell out with Warwickshire and Peter Cranmer took over, while neighbouring Worcestershire offered Cyril Walters the position of secretary with which he combined the job of captain. A delightful batsman, Walters dropped out of the first-class game through ill-health, and Hon. C.J. Lyttleton, later Lord Cobham, succeeded him.

Lyttleton was the last representative of what we have called the amateur spirit. He hit lustily, and often effectively, and played with a zest and abandon which endeared him to his team and to the onlookers. In 1938, when Bradman's Australians opened their tour at Worcester, he won the toss, but asked the Australians to bat first on a good wicket because he thought that people had paid to see the tourists bat. It was not a thing that Sellers, Robins or Jardine would have contemplated.

Another Midland county, Leicestershire, had been captained by E.W. Dawson and Hon. A.G. Hazelrigg, both Etonians, both capable batsmen, but after 1934, neither felt that they could give more time to the game. For several years, to quote *Wisden*, Leicestershire cricket 'entirely lacked distinction', and with no amateur available regularly in 1935, they appointed William Astill, a professional, as captain.

At the time, Leicestershire were a county with a poor record and financial problems. Under Astill, they enjoyed 'the most successful season in the history of the club', 'the presence of a regular and first-class leader undoubtedly led to a strong will-to-win spirit and provided just the fillip needed to set the club on its feet once more'.

'Virtually an all-professional side,' wrote *The Cricketer*, 'it was led with an urbanity and imperturbable ability by Astill. Inconspicuous in authority, he never seemed at fault when directing, and it is only just that a public dinner should afford testimony to this fine sportsman.' His leadership was outstanding, it was reported; but for 1936, C.S. Dempster, the fine New Zealand batsman, now qualified for Leicestershire and playing as an amateur, was appointed captain. Normal order had been re-established, but the taboo had been breached. Astill was the first professional to be appointed captain of a county club since Mordecai Sherwin had led Notts in 1888, and he had proved how well a professional could do the job. There was little time to ponder, however, for the Second World War was only three years away.

6 The Twilight of the Amateur

Leicestershire had broken with tradition when they appointed Astill captain in 1935, and they violated convention again in 1946 when, among the 17 first-class counties, they alone named a professional captain, Les Berry. They enjoyed their best season since the year of Astill's captaincy.

Berry was a delightful man. He was an opening batsman who would have played for England had he been associated with a more fashionable county, and he led the side with good humour and common sense. He gave way to Stuart Symington in 1949 who was 22 years old, the youngest post-war captain and who had made his début only the year before. A regular army officer, an amateur, Symington was a fair all-rounder who left first-class cricket after that one season of captaincy during which Leicestershire finished bottom of the table. He was replaced by Charles Palmer who came from Worcestershire to act as secretary-captain.

Palmer was a very useful all-rounder, his batting being his strength, and he proved a wise and popular leader who did much to lift Leicestershire from the doldrums after the reactionary appointment of Symington. Palmer's move to Leicestershire, however, was typical of much that was happening at the time, for whenever a county threatened to have a professional captain it seemed as if some higher authority found an amateur who could be imported and was capable of doing the job.

When first-class cricket resumed in 1946 the old order was accepted. Irrespective of any other considerations, a county had to be led by an amateur. Leicestershire were the only deviants. Whatever the political changes that were taking place in the country with the formation of the Welfare State, and however much the Second World

Full of fire, enthusiasm and inspiration – Walter Robins.

War had broken down former class barriers, those who administered cricket were determined that the game should continue as if nothing had disturbed it. They were succoured by the fact that people, starved of professional sporting entertainment for six years, flocked to watch cricket and football.

The supply of amateurs of first-class standing had been growing thin in the years before the war, and the dearth was even more marked in 1946. Veterans like Tom Pearce, J.C. Clay, Walter Robins, Valentine and Sellers were pressed into service while new men were introduced to first-class cricket with some bizarre results.

Northamptonshire lost their skipper, R.P. Nelson, during the war, and named Peter Murray-Willis as the Club Captain in 1946. He had played a handful of games for Worcestershire and Northants before the war, but his enthusiasm could not compensate for the several matches he was forced to miss through business calls and his deficiencies as a player, attested by his career batting average of 10.37.

The resignation of Murray-Willis led Northants to apply to Middlesex for the registration of Arthur Childs-Clarke whose ten first-class matches had been played over a period which had begun in 1923 and ended in 1934. He had done fine work as captain of Middlesex second eleven and was much respected, but Northants finished bottom of the table in the two years that he was their captain – although this was no novel experience for them.

The Northamptonshire revival came when Freddie Brown took over in 1949. Educated at The Leys, Cambridge, and at the university in the same city, Brown had enjoyed a fine career in his undergraduate days. Originally a leg-break and googly bowler and hard-hitting batsman, he had done the 'double' in his first full season of county cricket for Surrey and had been chosen for the tour of Australia in 1932–3 with Jardine's team. He had taken no part in the Test series, and his career in the years before the war followed the pattern of so many amateurs of the time, a handful of appearances each season which scarcely brought him before the public eye nor rekindled memories of his great all-round season. He spent three years as a prisoner of war and between 1946 and 1948 made one solitary reappearance for Surrey in the Championship so that, to all intents and purposes, now 39 years old, his career was over.

There was, however, concern for events at Northamptonshire. Captaincy was seen as the main cause of the County's problems. Murray-Willis and Childs-Clarke were admirable men in many ways, but neither had the experience to bind together a band of professionals, many of them very able, who seemed beaten before they went on the pitch. Some saw there being a danger of Northants becoming an all-professional side, for certainly in Brookes they had a player capable of leading such a side. This solution to the County's problems was averted when Freddie Brown accepted a business appointment in Northampton, was specially registered for the County and agreed to take charge of the team. What kind of business appointment it was that allowed him to play cricket both summer and winter one can only surmise.

Brown's presence transformed Northants. He himself did the 'double' for the second time in his career, the County played with zest and rose to sixth in the table. By the end of the 1949 season, Brown was also captain of England. Yardley had given way to George Mann because of business pressures, but Mann's own lively career was cut short for the same reason, so, after a twelve-year absence from Test cricket, Brown was recalled as captain.

With neither Yardley nor Mann available and Edrich out of favour, Brown was invited to lead England in Australia in 1950–51. He had revitalised Northamptonshire cricket and although he was not to have quite the same success with England, he did much to restore prestige and rekindle spirit. He had a zest for the game and was brimful of courage and endeavour. His side did not enjoy the best of luck, at one time injury reduced the team to three bowlers, but they ran Australia close before winning the final Test. It was England's first victory over Australia since 1938.

Brown took England to victory over a moderate South African side the following summer and retired as captain of Northants in 1953 in which season, as chairman of Test selectors, he was persuaded to return to Test cricket for one match against Australia. But by then England had a professional captain.

The desire to preserve the status of the amateur as captain was clearly demonstrated at Northants where, when Murray-Willis or Childs-Clarke was not available, A.C.L. Bennett was often asked to play and captain the side. Leo Bennett was a noted club cricketer with the BBC where his work prevented him from appearing regularly in first-class cricket, but when he did manage to play it was invariably as captain.

There are those who believe that it was intended that he should be captain of Surrey in 1946, for he had been educated at Dulwich and lived in the county. The man who was appointed to lead Surrey in 1946 was Nigel Harvie Bennett, a club cricketer with Brondesbury and Maoris.

Of all the appointments of county captains in an effort to maintain the amateur tradition, this ranks among the strangest. There was an apocryphal story in the 1950s and 1960s that the Surrey Committee, in search of a captain, had decided to offer the job to Leo Bennett and that Nigel Bennett went to The Oval to take out membership of the Club but was mistaken for Leo and offered the captaincy. This is a cruel jest, but it emphasises how little was known of N.H. Bennett when he was appointed captain of one of the greatest counties in 1946.

Surrey had suffered more than most during the war. The playing area in 1945 was in need of a complete overhaul, and the pavilion had been damaged by bombing. H.M. Garland-Wells, captain in 1939, had been badly wounded and did not feel capable of leading the side again. His predecessor, Errol Holmes, an exciting cricketer, gave his time entirely to work for the Surrey Restoration Fund and did not feel that he could play cricket as well. Given these problems, Surrey's appointment of Bennett was still a strange one, for very little was known of the man.

In the Spring Annual of *The Cricketer*, 1946, Norman Preston could write:

Several of the Surrey professionals met for the first time their new

> captain, N.H. Bennett, at the opening of the East Hill Cricket School, run by A. Sandham and A.R. Gover. Born on September 23, 1912, at Walton-on-Thames, Bennett has never figured in first-class cricket but he is known in London club circles as a hard-hitting batsman. In 1930, he headed the Stowe batting, while in 1936 he appeared in the county second team. During the war he has served in the Far East, rising to the rank of Major in the Royal Engineers. I am told he has a pleasing personality and when he settles down he should make plenty of runs.

Bennett had played five innings for Surrey second eleven in 1936, but he was not well known in club circles. Leo Bennett's book, *The Week-end Cricketer*, published in 1951 and listing, one feels, everyone of note who had played club cricket in south-east England at that time, makes no mention of him.

One can only admire N.H. Bennett's courage in accepting the position of Surrey captain although one feels he cannot have anticipated how difficult the task would be. The County had lost its complete stock of towels and other equipment during the military occupation of The Oval and extra clothing coupons were needed to replace these and to kit out the players. Each player was granted 15 extra coupons, but these were hardly sufficient for the purpose of buying flannels, shirts, blazers, towels and socks. Bennett, instantly capped, was seen wearing a 'real pre-war Surrey blazer' which had belonged to R. de W.K. Winlaw whose relatives had returned it to the Oval when he was killed in a flying accident. It was an innocent act for the new captain to wear the blazer, but it was one that was hardly likely to be well received by a group of hardened professionals who, if not hostile, were at least sceptical.

Fishlock, Barling, Gregory, Parker, Squires, Mobey, Watts and Gover were seasoned campaigners who made Surrey a very hard side to beat in the years before the war when Bennett himself had been in New Zealand for business reasons. Not only did he have little understanding of the county game, but he had been out of touch with it for several years. As a cricketer he did not fare too badly, hitting 605 championship runs in the lower order and taking the wicket of Haydn Davies of Glamorgan on one of the three occasions on which he bowled. It should, perhaps, be added that Glamorgan needed only two to win in their second innings, and Davies, usually at number ten opened and lost his wicket to Bennett who had elected to bowl what all believed would be the one and only over. As a captain, however, he had a disastrous time.

It was soon apparent that he had little knowledge of the game and little control over the senior professionals. Those who played against Surrey at the time remember it as an embarrassing experience. There appeared to be several captains on the field. Orders were barked from all directions. Decisions were made and rescinded. It was not a happy time.

Wisden commented on Bennett's predicament. He found 'want of knowledge of county cricket on the field presented an unconquerable hindrance to the satisfactory accomplishment of arduous duties. This prejudiced the general work of the side, and several bad spells culminated in consecutive defeats in the last six Championship matches.' Surrey finished twelfth in the table, a position that was unacceptable. Errol Holmes, captain from 1934 to 1938, agreed to take up that position again.

This obsession with looking at the social status of a candidate for captaincy rather than at the man himself and his ability to cope with a difficult job at a difficult time cost counties dear. Les Berry, at Leicestershire, being a professional, was hampered by the fact that the committee refused to appoint him on a permanent basis for the 1946 season. He was captain on a week to week basis as it were, with those in authority presumably nursing the hope that an acceptable amateur might still arrive. What all were looking for were amateurs who could hit a thousand runs or take a hundred wickets a season while possessing an astute tactical knowledge, an attractive personality and the capacity to inspire others. Such men were not too numerous. Sometimes counties were blinded by a man's limitations as a player and failed to see his value as a captain.

In 1946, Lancashire found themselves in a position similar to that of Surrey. Old Trafford had been bombed in 1941, and the pavilion had been damaged and the field of play pitted with craters. Peter Eckersley, who had given up a political career to captain Lancashire between 1929 and 1935 and then given up cricket to concentrate on politics, had been killed in the early days of the war. W.H.L. Lister, who had succeeded Eckersley, felt unable to resume first-class cricket. The energetic Tom Higson, the driving force behind the efforts to re-establish the County after the ravages of war, could not afford the time to play, and the excellent all-rounder Jack Iddon was mentioned as a likely captain. He was a professional, but it was believed that he would turn amateur so that he could lead the County. Tragically, he was killed in a car crash early in 1946.

As new players were enrolled to bolster the playing staff, the new captain appointed was J.A. Fallows. He was 39 years old and the son of the club treasurer. His experience was limited to club cricket and to a few appearances for Cheshire in 1932 when he met with very limited success. He had lost the services of some of the Club's most experienced players, including Oldfield, Paynter and Farrimond who, for various reasons, had declined the terms that they were offered, and he took up his post amid much criticism. In his first match, against Cambridge University at Fenner's, he delayed a declaration and was again 'at the centre of controversy'. By the end of the season, criticism had vanished.

Jack Fallows was not good enough for first-class cricket. He invariably batted in the last three or four, hit 151 Championship runs, average 5.39, and did not bowl, yet his contribution to Lancashire cricket was immense.

'One thing was clear: under J.A. Fallows the old stigmas of dullness and lack of imagination were overcome. Whatever his limitations as a batsman, the new captain proved shrewd in the field and inspiring everywhere. Willingness to go out for victory and keen finishes ensured maximum interest and enjoyment.'

Wisden's enthusiasm was justified. Failing narrowly to beat Essex and Hampshire at Old Trafford in August when set to make runs against the clock cost Lancashire the title, and they finished third to Yorkshire and Middlesex.

It was a time of austerity. Travelling, hotel accommodation and food rationing all presented problems, but Fallows led his men cheerfully up and down the land, moulding them into a happy fighting unit and overcoming all difficulties. On the field, he sought the advice of Washbrook and Pollard, his senior professionals, and he set an example with some excellent fielding. Off the field, he showed concern for his team at all times, making hotel accommodation more comfortable and conjuring food from hidden sources. In his history of Lancashire, John Kay told how Fallows made light of the most pressing problems.

> He excelled himself one morning in a certain London hotel when, with only four fresh eggs available for twelve players and a scorer, he ended all arguments with the wisdom of a Solomon. 'We are in the field this morning. Let the bowlers have the eggs . . . the batsmen can have them tomorrow.' A simple solution, yet an important one, and typical of Fallows at all times!

Fallows had given Lancashire panache and they were feared by all in the country. Yorkshire were fortunate to escape defeat in the August Bank Holiday game at Old Trafford which, with both counties in contention for the title, roused tremendous interest. The players were happy. The crowds were flocking excitedly to Old Trafford. Lancashire finished third; and Fallows was sacked.

Just as the season ended, Fallows learned through a leak to the press that he was to be replaced by Ken Cranston. Naturally, he was both shocked and hurt. So were the players. Cranston was a good all-rounder, good enough to play Test cricket, but he had experience of neither captaincy nor man management. He was on good terms with the professionals, but he was not encouraged to seek their advice, and there was a suggestion of manipulation from the committee room. A rift developed between those who played and those who administered which was to widen with the years until it was to break into an open hostility which surprised only those who had been unaware of events.

Fallows was to return as committee man and chairman of selectors in the 1960s, but it took till then to heal Lancashire's problems.

Cranston left cricket to concentrate on his dental practice, and Lancashire appointed Nigel Howard in his place. The obvious choice for captain was Cyril Washbrook, an experienced and knowledgeable cricketer who was well respected by all. But, though he had just enjoyed a large benefit, he showed no inclination to become an amateur, the price required if he were to become captain of Lancashire.

N.D. Howard was 24 years old, a very promising, attractive right-handed batsman. That he never fulfilled that promise was due entirely to the fact that he was burdened by a position and a situation that would have tried the greatest of cricketers.

There were some very unkind things written about Howard's period of captaincy, and most of them were related to the fact that it was the club chairman and the club secretary who were making the decisions. John Kay relates a tale which may or may not be true, but which was typical of the rumours current at the time.

> Indeed, he was often the recipient of messages and telegrams at home and away, containing instructions about what to do if he won the toss and when to make bowling changes. On one occasion a careless telephonist misheard and Howard received a telegram advising him to 'put Greenwood in first'. He duly did so, when what was meant was 'put Greenwood on first'. A distinction with a difference, and a state of affairs that could not help any cricketing cause.

The professionals remained loyal to him, knowing where the real fault was rooted, and, to his credit, Howard battled on and introduced exciting young players like Statham and Tattersall, but the Lancashire cricket, whether winning or losing, had lost its zest. He did not spare himself in his county's cause and was ever encouraging of the young, but he was thrust into a position for which he was ill-equipped in age and experience, and it was sad that a player who had promised so much talent felt it necessary to retire from the game at the age of 28.

His selection as captain of the MCC side to tour India in 1951–2 highlighted the problem that was confronting England in maintaining the tradition of amateur captaincy, and it was not the happiest of tours. Howard played his four Test matches as England's captain and was then unfortunate in contracting pleurisy. His form was poor in 1952 and he stood down from the Lancashire side on occasions, with Washbrook taking over.

In spite of growing discontent among supporters and falling membership, he was retained as captain for 1953, but at the end of that season he announced his retirement. Few men have struggled on so bravely against the odds.

Lancashire broke with tradition and named Washbrook, a professional, as captain, but the appointment had come five years too late. He had learned his cricket in that stern era of the 1930s when the young professional accepted his place in the scheme of things. By the time he took over as Lancashire captain, those ideas were becoming undermined by cricketers new to the game who refused to accept what they saw as an outdated feudal system. They were assertive, casual and high-spirited. They were not of Washbrook's generation, and he was able to find no meeting ground with them. As a committee member, he has rigidly adhered to old principles, and it is mainly due to his insistence that ladies are still not admitted to the pavilion at Old Trafford.

He led Lancashire until 1959, his efforts not always appreciated by the supporters of the Club who still looked for more flair and for better results from a side of undoubted talent. The ideal successor to Washbrook would have been Geoffrey Edrich who had been put in charge of the second eleven and had had considerable influence on the development of several fine young cricketers, but Edrich had been dismissed in 1958 after some of his second-eleven players had become too excited on an away trip. He refused to name the culprits, took the responsibility himself as captain and was dismissed. In fairness, it should be added that he was, by then, 40 years old, only four years younger than Washbrook whom he would have replaced.

Lancashire now committed the same error that they had done with Howard a decade earlier. They turned to a talented young amateur, Bob Barber. Barber was 24, a thrilling left-handed opening batsman and a capable leg-break bowler. He faced a difficult task in an atmosphere of veiled hostility, and his position was made even worse when it was decided to return to the system of the 1930s and have the captain and other amateurs stay in one hotel and the professionals in another when the side was on tour. It was just as if there had been no Second World War, no 14 years of change since that war and no Hutton as captain of England. Barber was a sad, lonely cricketer. He had little authority and little understanding of the professional cricketer, and he failed to seek advice from his senior men.

In 1960 Lancashire vied with Yorkshire for the Championship, but the season ended in bitterness and rancour. At Old Trafford at the beginning of August, Barber set Kent to make 334 in four and a half hours, but they made no attempt to score the runs. Barber responded, unwisely, by launching a severe and public attack on the captaincy of Colin Cowdrey. He was reprimanded by his committee. Dyson, a useful all-rounder, was sacked. Clayton, a good wicket-keeper, but a turbulent spirit, was dropped and was sacked four years later after more dissension. Wharton moved to Leicestershire. The season ended with Barber and his professionals in a state of almost open warfare and a committee embarrassed by their captain's criticism of Cowdrey.

He led the side for one more season, his own skills suffering in the process, for he was a plainly unhappy man. It was announced that he was to be relieved of the captaincy for 1962, a decision which he accepted gracefully, although one more season convinced him that he had had enough of Lancashire cricket. He left to join Warwickshire where his talents came to full bloom at county and Test level.

In the north, Lancashire and Yorkshire are always gazing across the Pennines to see how the other is faring. While Lancashire were despairing Yorkshire were triumphing. Yorkshire had been revived by J.R. Burnet. He captained the second eleven for five years and then, in 1958, aged 40, he was appointed captain of the county side.

W.H.H. Sutcliffe, son of Herbert, had succeeded Yardley, but pressure of business forced him to stand down at the end of the 1957 season. Surrey had monopolised the Championship for seven years, which was not to Yorkshire's liking, and it was felt that a man of strong discipline was needed to take the White Rose back to that position of eminence which it saw as its birthright.

It was not until November 1957 that the committee decided to name Burnet as Sutcliffe's successor, and he first knew that he had been appointed when he read of it in a newspaper. The character of the man can clearly be discerned from the way in which he negotiated a traumatic beginning.

He was unknown outside Yorkshire, had no first-class experience, inherited a side which was far from united and had just lost the services of Watson who had moved to Leicestershire. Appleyard and Lowson, hampered by injury, were to leave at the end of the 1958 season. The weather was awful, and there was the Wardle affair.

Johnny Wardle was a slow left-arm bowler in the great Yorkshire tradition. His powers of spin were exceptional, and he took 102 Test wickets at moderate cost. He was, however, something of a caustic man, not averse to expressing forceful opinions both to captain and colleagues. The public saw only the jovial entertainer.

During the match with Somerset at Sheffield in late July, the

Lancashire captain Bob Barber bowling against Warwickshire in 1962. His future Warwickshire and English captain, Mike Smith, is the non-striking batsman.

Yorkshire secretary announced that the County would not be calling on the services of Wardle after the end of the 1958 season. The announcement shattered the cricket world, unaware of events behind the scenes. Burnet issued a statement before the Roses match at Old Trafford saying that Wardle had asked to stand down from the side because of comments he intended to make in a newspaper article to be published during the match and that permission had been granted and Wardle had left the ground.

Articles duly appeared in the *Daily Mail* in which Wardle made unflattering comments about his team-mates, his captain, the coaches and the committee. The Yorkshire committee responded with a dignified statement which made clearer their reasons for dismissing

Wardle, saying that he had been warned on several occasions as to his behaviour on the field and in the dressing-room, but that as no improvement had been shown, it had been decided unanimously to dispense with his services. The newspaper articles constituted a breach of agreement, and his contract was terminated forthwith. Moreover, in the wake of Wardle's action, the invitation that had been issued to him to tour Australia with Peter May's side was withdrawn. His county and Test careers were at an end.

Yorkshire took their action in the belief that 'it was essential to have discipline and a happy and loyal team before any lasting improvement could be expected in the play of the Yorkshire XI'. Wardle was later to say that he was sacked because he 'refused to accept the authority of the hopeless old man appointed captain', but he received no support from his colleagues who issued an unsolicited statement pledging their loyalty to, and confidence in, Burnet.

Burnet began his second season of captaincy, 1959, under a cloud of disapproval and grumbling from supporters for whom recent events had been unsavoury, smacking of a desire to preserve a fading order. He ended the year as a hero. After an uneasy start Yorkshire climbed towards the top of the table in July, but they lost ground in August, and it was a late surge which took them to the title. They reached Hove in the last two days of August and the first of September needing to win to claim the Championship.

The match against Sussex will long be remembered in cricket history. Sussex made 210, and Yorkshire, with Illingworth, who did the 'double' in all matches, hitting a hundred, made 307. By lunch time on the last day, Sussex led by 183 and had three wickets standing. There was no question of a declaration, for Robin Marlar, the Sussex captain, was always a strict adherer to the basic principles of the game which demanded that no side in Yorkshire's position should be granted any favours.

Half an hour after lunch, Sussex were all out for 311, and Yorkshire were left with the massive task of scoring 218 runs in 95 minutes if they were to win the Championship. Stott hit 13 of the 15 obtained from Thomson's opening over. Fifty was on the board in 20 minutes. The hundred came up in 43 minutes. Stott hit 96 in 86 minutes, and he and Padgett added 141 for the third wicket in just over an hour. With seven minutes remaining, Bolus deflected a ball from Dexter to the fine leg boundary, and Yorkshire had won, thus ending Surrey's seven-year reign as champions.

Burnet resigned at the end of the season. His two years in first-class cricket had brought him 897 runs, average 12.63, but his contribution to Yorkshire cricket can never be measured in terms of the runs he scored. 'Always he had to live down the accusation,' wrote *Wisden*, 'that his own form was weakening the side, but eventually, because of his personality and ability to get the utmost from the men under him, he received due recognition as an important figure in the Yorkshire revival.'

Yorkshire at last bowed to the changing times, and Vic Wilson, the senior professional, was named as Burnet's successor. In many ways, Burnet represented the amateur captain's last fling.

If Yorkshire could find revival through a man like Burnet, why not Lancashire? To succeed Barber they chose Joseph Frederick Blackledge. He had played occasionally for Lancashire second eleven and had done quite well in the Northern League. He was 34 years old and was said to have a flair for the game.

Burnet had known the men whom he was to lead at Yorkshire; Blackledge did not and first had to be introduced to the Lancashire side already disgruntled at recent history. As the season wore on things became worse. Lancashire endured the worst period in their history until that time, and Blackledge, a modest performer, was subjected to most of the criticism. He was no inspiration in the field where he often laboured, but he should receive sympathy rather than condemnation, for he had been grotesquely miscast by people who should have known better. They seemed to have little idea of what leadership in first-class cricket entailed, and the effect on the side was devastating. In attempting to emulate Yorkshire, Lancashire had failed to grasp the understanding of the basis on which Burnet had been appointed. Blackledge expressed a wish to be relieved of his post.

We have concentrated our attention on the north. Let us now turn back to the south where the tradition of the amateur captain was strong. Sussex broke with that tradition in 1950 when James Langridge, the senior professional, was appointed captain. A loyal and professionally dedicated man, he led the side unobtrusively, but a new breed of distinguished Oxbridge cricketers appeared to take up the reins again.

Neighbouring Hampshire made an inspired choice in 1946 when they persuaded Desmond Eagar to come from Gloucestershire and act as captain and joint secretary. Eagar had first played for Gloucestershire when at Cheltenham and had gone up to Oxford where he gained his blue in 1939. He had done nothing exceptional before he joined Hampshire, but in his eleven years as skipper of the south coast side he worked tirelessly to turn Hampshire into a most entertaining team, backed by sound organisation and financial stability. An inspiration on the field, he brought vitality to a ponderous side and passed on to his successor, Colin Ingleby-Mackenzie, the nucleus of the team that was to win the Championship in 1961.

Ingleby-Mackenzie was a throw-back to the Edwardian amateur or to Tennyson, except that he had a sympathy and understanding of the professionals under him and was an excellent man-manager. He cut a romantic figure as a swashbuckling left-handed batsman who lived well and liked a gamble and whose only rule for his championship-winning side was said to be 'Be in bed by breakfast time.' It was an image that the public and press found attractive, but he also had determination and a sharp brain, as his subsequent business career would indicate.

The need for the captain to be an amateur was still seen as obligatory by most counties, and the tradition certainly motivated the actions of some. Bill Edrich returned from the 1946–7 tour of Australia, where he had been senior professional in Hammond's side, and announced that he had taken up a business appointment which would allow him to play as an amateur in future. Most people interpreted this as a bid for the England captaincy. Hammond had retired, and Norman Yardley, his vice-captain, was under great pressure.

Yardley was an excellent captain, a kind, strong, thoughtful and sympathetic man who did much with limited resources, but he had lost his best years to the war and his post-war form never touched the heights of his pre-war excellence with the bat. He was also deeply involved with the family business which took much of his time. George Mann, 'Gubby' Allen and Freddie Brown deputised for Yardley during his tenure of office (1947–50), but only Brown could subsequently give himself unrestrainedly to the job.

In 1947 Edrich was 31. He had been a Squadron Leader and won the DFC in the war. He and Compton, in that summer of 1947, formed the most exciting batting partnership that the game has ever known. He was also a fine fielder and, for a short period, as brisk a bowler as any in the country, admittedly in a bleak period. He had all the attributes, seemingly, to take over the captaincy of England; yet even Middlesex were reluctant to give him the post in succession to Mann and Robins. He was first asked to share the captaincy with Compton, a most unhappy experiment, and then held office without ever seeming to have the full backing of the committee. At Test level, the honour never came his way.

Two reasons can be offered for this although both are conjecture. Firstly, although a lively and warm companion, he tended to become cold and formal when he spoke publicly and presented a character in complete contrast to the man he was. Secondly, he avowed that he suffered a three-year ban from Test cricket although no statement was issued to this effect. Edrich maintained that a selector had seen him return to his hotel room in the early hours of the morning following a party during the England – West Indies Test match at Lord's in 1950, the occasion when England were beaten by West Indies for the first time in a Test in England. Nothing was said, but he was not chosen for England until 1953, three years and a week after the Lord's defeat. His non-selection for the party that Freddie Brown led to Australia in 1950–51 was certainly a major surprise, but one feels that he never figured prominently in anybody's mind regarding captaincy in spite of the fact that he had made himself available and was the one candidate who could be seen as having a valid place in the side.

The amateur monopolisation of captaincy had been broken, however. There had been two excursions at Leicester, both short-lived, but the significant appointment came at Edgbaston in 1949. Peter Cranmer had returned to lead Warwickshire for the first two post-war seasons, and he had stepped down in 1948 when the side was led jointly by Ron Mauldsley and Tom Dollery.

Mauldsley was an Oxford don who was employed at the University teaching Law until mid-June. He was named as captain, no other amateur being willing to undertake the job, with Dollery, the professional, leading the side in the first twelve matches until Mauldsley became available. Dollery was conscious of the controversy that his appointment would cause although the sharing of the captaincy with Mauldsley the official head covered the event with a smoke-screen.

Warwickshire enjoyed a good season, but it was recognised that to divide the captaincy was not a sound policy. The Committee Report stressed, 'The team achieved a great success in the early part of last season and towards the end; a rather less successful time was during the middle of the season immediately after the changeover. Such a change inevitably has an unsettling effect on a team as a composite force.' Mauldsley himself was behind this statement. He stated that he was unable to captain the side throughout the 1949 season and that he did not wish to be considered as a candidate for the captaincy although he would like to assist the county whenever they would like to call on him. Inevitably, Dollery was named as captain.

The press gave a mixed reception to the appointment, but the *Birmingham Post* gave support:

> Our grandfathers might well have looked in pained surprise at even the notion of a professional leading a county side, but thank goodness we have advanced far since the days the amateurs and professionals left the pavilion by different gates. It is the game which counts and if a man is a good sportsman, a first-class cricketer, a born leader and appeals to the crowd, then he is the man to skipper the team . . . We have every confidence in the new skipper.

Dollery was aware that the principal objections to the professional as captain were that he was likely to be too cautious in his methods, would be dominated by the Committee and would be unable to command his fellow professionals effectively. In fact, Dollery was a most positive leader although he was never foolhardy. He had been appointed by a sound and wise committee who had thought long and been unanimous in their appointment, and, as we have already noted, being an amateur captain did not preclude one from committee domination at other counties like Lancashire. His fellow professionals saw themselves as well as Dollery being on trial, and they were out to prove to the cricket world that they could manage their own affairs like all mature and responsible men.

Dollery was to write later:

> It would not be true to say that the professionals have been embittered by the years of discrimination which lasted in the most acute form right up to 1939 – the companionship of the cricket field has prevented that, with the knowledge that many amateurs disliked the use of separate dressing-rooms and separate gates even more than we did. But it would not have been in human nature to have been unaffected by it.

Dollery himself remembered the pre-war days when the professionals crowded into one small room and the amateurs, or amateur, had the use of a spacious dressing-room, and he believed that when he was appointed captain fellow professionals saw this as 'us being on the point of removing the last great disability of professionalism'.

All this might have passed unnoticed had not Warwickshire, under Dollery, proved to be a dynamic team. They finished fourth in 1949 and 1950 and took the title in 1951. Only one amateur, E.B. Lewis, appeared in their Championship-winning side, and he played in only one match.

Wisden, in 1952, listed Dollery as one of the 'Five Cricketers of the Year', saying that he was a man:

> able to get the best out of his team both on and off the field. Dollery, a professional, led an all-professional eleven, and while twentieth-century conditions rob the game of the real amateur Dollery showed the paid player can become a captain in the real sense of the word. By his astute work, Dollery has raised the status of the professional just as Hobbs did in the days when every county had one dressing-room for the paid and another for the unpaid.

The demarcation between amateurs and professionals had been broken down at Lord's during the war, in fact, when, in those

Tom Dollery.

wonderfully entertaining games, changing accommodation was simply *home* and *away*. The professionals' room had been at the end of the pavilion next to the Warner Stand. A small bar has now replaced it. 'Even so,' wrote Dollery, 'professionals still feel some inferiority, as was made clear when we had won the championship by the many professionals, whether still in active cricket or retired, who hailed the victory as a great vindication of professionalism.'

The success of Dollery and Warwickshire had made it clear that it was the man himself not an artificial distinction that made a good captain, but Dollery was too sane a person to believe that the break-through had been complete. He knew that the weight of establishment opinion was still heavily against the idea of a professional captain and that he had to tread warily. In the year that

Warwickshire won the title, Nottinghamshire had met Glamorgan at Trent Bridge and the visitors had batted so slowly on the first day that Reg Simpson, the Notts captain, had put himself on to bowl and bowled an over of lobs as a protest. Robin Marlar of Sussex and Wilf Wooller carried out similar actions at other times, but Dollery noted that there was still 'sufficient prejudice for behaviour which, in an amateur, would be attributed to a sense of humour or eccentricity, to be called "bad taste" if it were to come from a professional'.

Others were to follow Dollery as professional captains. His successor at Warwickshire was Eric Hollies while Perks and Kenyon, who did a splendid job, led Worcestershire. Dennis Brookes took over from Freddie Brown at Northants, and Leicestershire imported Willie Watson from Yorkshire to lead them. Maurice Tremlett was successful and popular at Somerset where he is still remembered with the greatest affection, as is his successor Harold Stephenson.

The changes that were effected at county level were as nothing, however, in comparison to the revolutionary break with tradition that occurred at Test level in 1952. The England captaincy had begun to give cause for concern. Hammond had retired. Neither Yardley nor Mann could give themselves fully to the game, and Brown was ageing. There had been five other amateurs in the side that he took to Australia in 1950–51, Bailey, Simpson, Sheppard, Warr and Dewes, but the Test careers of Warr and Dewes ended with that tour, Sheppard was comparatively young and untried, and neither Bailey nor Simpson was forwarded as a likely candidate for the England captaincy. Indeed, in spite of the presence of five amateurs as well as the captain on the 1950–51 tour, Denis Compton had been named as Brown's deputy, and there was some speculation, as he shared the captaincy of Middlesex with Edrich, that he might succeed Brown.

An historic change had been brought about in 1950 when Leslie Ames had been made a member of the selection committee, for no professional had been accorded such an honour before, and if tradition could be broken at committee level, then there was reason to suppose it could be broken on the field. Yet Compton was hardly likely to be the one to change the pattern by becoming England's first professional captain for 70 years. He was immensely popular, but one of his charms was an aura of innocent irresponsibility that he exuded, and this was hardly a recommendation for Test captaincy. Moreover, his form in Australia had been dreadful, and he had become increasingly troubled by the knee injury which restricted his mobility.

Ames, and his fellow selectors Yardley (the chairman), Wyatt and Brown, faced a dilemma regarding the captaincy. Nigel Howard, as we have noted, took the MCC side to India with Donald Carr as his deputy, but the team was dubbed a 'second eleven' before it went and the results, both on and off the field, were not encouraging.

On his return from Australia in 1951, Len Hutton, England's leading batsman along with Denis Compton, was sounded out as to whether or not he would consider becoming an amateur with the prospect of the England captaincy as a bait. But Hutton was a true and honest Yorkshire professional who could see no reason for changing his status.

There were wider issues than the England captaincy which, if not the direct concern of the selectors, must temper any decisions that they were to make. There was a general pessimism concerning the future of the game. It had not come to terms with the changed financial situation, for crowds were dropping, and there were pleas for brighter cricket. What was desperately needed was for England to climb to the top again and rekindle interest, as Chapman's side had done in 1926. The MCC side against the Indian tourists in May 1952 was led by Trevor Bailey, and a large crowd turned up at Lord's on the Saturday to see an entertaining first day. Bailey was not a front runner for the England captaincy. *The Cricketer*, voicing the opinion of many, thought that the selectors had two choices, either to choose an experienced cricketer as captain simply for the series against India or to choose a younger man and blood him with a view to leading the side against Australia the following year. The man most often mentioned if the selectors opted for the second course was David Sheppard, in his last year at Cambridge where he was captain. In the event, they invited Len Hutton to captain the side in the first Test at Headingley.

It was not a decision that pleased everybody, and few were as balanced as Geoffrey Green in *The Times*:

> For the first time a professional player has been chosen to captain England. Though there are many who will look back with anxious eyes and with sorrow at the passing of an age, there are yet those who will welcome the ending of an anachronism. The amateur, in the older meaning of the word, no longer truly exists. He has largely been destroyed by the economic circumstances of the mid-twentieth century. Further, to find such a man, both with the character to lead and also the quality to hold indisputably a place in an England team, has progressively become more difficult. When F.R. Brown was called on by the selectors two years ago the writing was on the wall. Brown's unqualified success, heartening though it was, solved nothing. It merely postponed the hour that was to come.
>
> The selectors, who for some time have been struggling to balance the requirements of tradition with the needs of the moment, are to be congratulated on the action they have taken.

Len Hutton and Cyril Washbrook.

In this age of so-called equal opportunity for all the professional player has at last attained his fullest stature, and it is now up to Hutton to prove not only himself but also his colleagues worthy of the new principle which has been established.

Even Green's welcome is shadowed by doubt, although one would have felt that Dollery had already proved the professionals' point. Hutton could not have been helped by the debate that his appointment had aroused, nor by the fact that the selectors approved him only for the first Test. The traditionalists comforted themselves by the belief that he was merely being used as a stop-gap until one of the young amateurs was able to take over.

Hutton proved his point. England won the first Test by seven wickets and failed to win only the last of the four Tests which was ruined by rain. Hutton, leading throughout the series, finished top of the Test match averages. The first Test had set an exciting pattern when, on the Saturday afternoon, India began their second innings and lost four wickets in 14 balls without a run being scored. Freddie Trueman, making his Test début, was the hero of the hour, and it seemed that England had found a captain and a fast bowler in the same match.

Even in the final, rain-ruined Test, England were exhilarating. Hutton and Sheppard put on 143 for the first wicket, and Trueman and Bedser reduced India to 6 for 5. There was bounding confidence in English cricket again, particularly as only a few months earlier India had beaten England in a Test match for the first time.

If those who paid to watch the game were happy, the hierarchy remained a little troubled, and one suspects that things had not gone quite as they had anticipated. *Wisden* dulled the enthusiasm with misgivings.

> In breaking with tradition and choosing a professional as captain the Selection Committee made a vital decision in the interests of England, because it should mean that in future no man will be picked as leader unless he is worth a place in the side.
>
> On the other hand, the time may not be far distant when England will have an amateur in charge again if P.B.H. May and D.S. Sheppard continue to improve. The task of captain is seldom a sinecure, and for a professional it could be onerous if disciplinary action was necessary against a fellow professional.

Norman Preston, the editor of *Wisden*, had again raised the worry caused by the equality of status and added a further caution when he wondered if Hutton would be bold enough when the opportunity presented itself against the Australians, for he did not want to see a repetition of the tactics that Hutton had employed when the Indians had been beaten by eight wickets at Lord's. Those tactics were that England, needing 77 to win, began their second innings with 80 minutes of the fourth day remaining. They lost Simpson at eight, and they ended the day on 40 for 1. Preston maintained that this was a tactical error, and Hutton should have pressed for victory that evening even though there were no doubts as to the weather.

To such a barrage of criticism and undermining was Hutton constantly subjected, but he was virtually unopposed to lead England against Australia in 1953. The weather ruined England's chances of winning the first Test. They needed 187 to win with nine wickets in hand and two days to spare, but rain prevented any further play until 4.30 on the last afternoon.

Defeat seemed imminent in the second Test, but Watson and Bailey batted throughout much of the last day to save the game. Australia had an embarrassment at Old Trafford when they were 35 for 8 in their second innings of a match destroyed by rain. At Headingley, they neeeded 177 in 115 minutes, but their violent hitting was halted by Bailey's leg theory. At The Oval, England won a memorable victory by eight wickets and with it the Ashes. Hutton's standing was close to what Chapman's had been in 1926.

He now took England to the West Indies and led his side back from two Test defeats to level the series. Hutton scored 205 in the fifth Test. But the tour had its problems. There was the bottle-throwing incident when the local crowd were angered by an umpiring decision, and England players, too, showed dissent at times. Off the field, there were diplomatic incidents and complaints as to the behaviour of some of the England party. From a distance of 34 years, they seem trivial blemishes in comparison to more recent events, but they were serious enough at the time. There were suggestions that Hutton was to blame, that a professional captain could be tolerated at home, but not on tour when social graces were needed.

Pakistan were playing their first Test series in England in 1954, and Hutton was unwell. He played in the first Test, but could not play in the second and third Tests, and David Sheppard was brought in to lead the side, in spite of the presence of May, Bailey, Simpson, Compton, Bedser and Graveney. Sheppard was a fine batsman and, as he has since proved as Bishop of Liverpool, a man of integrity, sympathy, intelligence and understanding. He had captained Sussex the previous season, but he had now begun to concentrate his life more fully on his ministry.

The selectors, Harry Altham, Wyatt, Ames and Robins, were all from the south, and when it seemed that Sheppard was being groomed to take the side to Australia at the end of the season instead of Hutton there was a verbal civil war. It appeared that Robins was pressing for Sheppard to be captain instead of Hutton, and, as we indicated earlier, Robins was not the most discreet of men. Indeed, he could be brutal in his utterances.

Debate raged in the press, and there was even an opinion poll conducted which came down heavily in favour of Hutton. But the prospect of Sheppard leading England to Australia excited those who had seen the appointment of a professional captain as only a temporary evil.

In fact, Hutton returned for the fourth Test, captained the side to Australia and retained the Ashes with Tyson and Statham the heroes. Sheppard did not go on the tour, which in effect marked the end of Hutton's career, for he played only a handful of games in 1955 when Peter May took over as England's captain.

The way of the pioneer is never easy, and for Hutton it was harder than we can have realised. Always under pressure as England's leading batsman, he had the added pressure of being a captain whose every move was constantly under scrutiny. In spite of his unparalleled success, he seemed ever to be on trial. Cautious by nature, he was made more cautious by circumstances, and although the symbol of a breaker of tradition, he was himself a traditionalist.

In spite of the achievements of Hutton at international level and Dollery at county level, the gate which had barred the professional's way to county captaincy did not open immediately. However violent a revolution, its objects are achieved only slowly, if at all.

Playing his second game for Glamorgan at the age of 17, with Hutton's reign as England's captain over and Dollery's championship-winning side four years in the past, Tony Lewis was led to the committee table for lunch in the match against Warwickshire by his captain Wilf Wooller, the only other amateur playing in the game. Lewis recalls that Wooller shouted, 'C'mon Tony. You'd better get used to the committee table. You'll be dealing a lot with them when you are captain.'

Tony Lewis was playing in only his second first-class match, having scored 0 and 9 in his first. National service and university lay ahead, but he was already marked down as captain, and, as he recollects, what Wooller was really saying was, 'As captain you can never be one of the boys. Start now.'

In fact, by the time Lewis became captain of Glamorgan, and then England, times had changed.

The west, like the south coast, took longer to accept the idea of a professional captain than most. To follow Wally Hammond and Basil Allen, Gloucestershire appointed Sir Derrick Bailey as captain in 1951. He was the only amateur in the side. The eldest son of the wealthy South African business man Sir Abe Bailey, who played for Transvaal, Sir Derrick Bailey was born in London in 1918, educated at Winchester and won the DFC when serving with the Royal South African Air Force during the war. Studying at the Royal Agricultural

College, Cirencester, after the war, he was persuaded to assist Gloucestershire on a few occasions in 1949 and two years later found himself captaining a side containing men like Graveney, Milton, Crapp, Young, Emmett, Goddard and Wilson.

He hit a thousand runs in his first season as captain, but *Wisden* remembered that his 'defensive stubbornness was worth more than its numerical value'.

His two years in office served, as with England and Brown, only to postpone the inevitable. The appointment of a professional captain was foreseen, but it was reluctantly accepted. The management committee was empowered to nominate a captain if they chose an amateur, but to report back to the council of the Club if they wanted to appoint a professional. Jack Crapp became the first professional captain of Gloucestershire in 1953, and he was followed by George Emmett and Tom Graveney.

Graveney took over the captaincy of Gloucestershire in 1959, and the County enjoyed a splendid season, finishing as runners up to Yorkshire. One of the most elegant batsmen in the country, Graveney was frequently absent due to injury, when Emmett and Milton shared the captaincy, but this seemed to have no detrimental effect on the team's form.

The following year was a disappointment in that Gloucestershire dropped to eighth in the championship table, but they were badly hit by injuries, including one to Graveney who carried a shoulder muscle strain for most of the season. The council, the main Gloucestershire committee, was split, however, some feeling that a professional captain was causing problems, that there was unrest in the dressing-room and that Graveney must go. The old guard was victorious, and in November, 1960 it was announced to an astonished cricket world that Tom Pugh would lead Gloucestershire the following season in place of Tom Graveney. As a consequence, one of the great delights of post-war cricket moved to Worcestershire, where he had further years of regal splendour.

The Gloucestershire committee obviously hoped that by appointing an amateur captain, an Old Etonian, with two years experience of first-class cricket, they would end all their problems. They were fighting against the current trend, and Pugh was to hold the post for only two years.

Middlesex, too, struggled to halt the incoming tide. Confronted by a captaincy problem after the retirement of the likeable and effective John Warr, they recalled Ian Bedford after an eight-year absence from the game. A man of great charm, he lacked the confidence to bowl his leg-breaks and the experience for a job which was becoming increasingly demanding. He was popular with his team, but slipped quietly out of first-class cricket after a couple of seasons.

He was luckier than Bill Murray-Wood whose captaincy of Kent ended abruptly in acrimony. A leg-break bowler and lower order batsman, he had played for Oxford against Cambridge in 1936, but was not in the side in the next two years. He made a few appearances for Kent before the war, but he was never a regular member of a side which, by the early 1950s, was one of the weakest counties in the championship.

Clark resigned as Kent captain in 1951, and it was hoped that Les Ames would succeed him. But Ames was 46 and did not feel fit enough to continue with the game, for he had long been troubled by a back injury. In fact, it has since been revealed that Ames had been offered the captaincy before Clark, but only if he would become an amateur, which he refused to do. Kent turned to Murray-Wood.

Murray-Wood had scored a century in his first first-class match in 1936, since when his cricket had steadily declined. He was a good fielder, but his leg-breaks were inaccurate, and his knowledge of the game and ability to manage men were hardly his strong points. From the start things did not go well for Kent under him, and it must be said that he was not always helped by some of his senior professionals. Tony Pawson recalls that in David Clark's time, Arthur Fagg had constantly grumbled that he was never consulted by the captain even though he was a senior professional. Pawson tactfully approached Clark who agreed readily to seek Fagg's advice on occasions. Next time Pawson passed Fagg, he heard him muttering, 'Always asking me what to do. He's supposed to be the bloody captain.' Murray-Wood's relationships with his team could not be dismissed with such light-hearted anecdotes.

In 1952, Kent were fifteenth in the Championship. They slipped one place lower in Murray-Wood's second year of captaincy, and from the start of the season, with unrest among the players growing, things went badly. In July the committee asked Murray-Wood to resign. He refused on the grounds that he had been appointed for the season. By Canterbury week, 1–7 August, the situation had become one of extreme tension. In the second match of the week, against Middlesex, there were rumours that the Kent players were refusing to take the field if Murray-Wood continued as captain. The committee was faced with the problem that they would be unable to raise sides to fulfil their last six fixtures. They took the unprecedented step of dismissing Murray-Wood in mid-season.

Unfortunately, but almost inevitably, the news of the committee decision was learned by the press before it was learned by the Kent captain and players. Sellers of evening papers were shouting the news on the ground at Canterbury before any official statement had been

Doug Wright – caretaker captain of a Kent side in a state of revolt.

made or any of those most closely involved with events had learned of what was to happen. Not unnaturally, there was much bitterness, and a decision which Kent had hoped could be taken with diplomacy and quietness was thrust into the full glare of publicity.

So many sorry tales surround the amateur captain in those dying years after the Second World War, yet there were some, like Burnet, who could reawaken memories of a golden past. One in particular stamped his name indelibly on cricket history.

Stuart Surridge first appeared for Surrey in a handful of matches in 1947. The following year he bowled with 'zest and profit'. He continued 'brimful with enthusiasm' and the County owed him much. By 1950, he was renowned as a splendid slip catcher who bowled his brisk medium with 'fire and effect'. His enthusiasm never waned and when M.R. Barton relinquished the Surrey captaincy at the end of the 1951 season Surridge was asked to take over.

He was blessed with a side which contained some outstanding cricketers, including Peter May, Laker, Lock, the Bedser twins and Alec McIntyre. But there have been oustanding players before and since who have never been welded into a Championship-winning side. Surridge captained Surrey for five seasons, and they won the Championship in each of those five seasons. It is a breath-taking record.

Frequently, Surrey were weakened by Test calls, but their eagerness to win, their positive approach to the game was never diminished. Surridge could see no point in being second, and he believed, and made his players believe, that Surrey could always bowl the other side out and could always reach a target, however worn the wicket.

Surrey played with consistent enterprise and aggression, but Surridge was no mere entertainer. His enthusiasm was to win, and his inspiration to his side sprang from that fact. Fielding close to the wicket, mostly on the off side with Lock patrolling the other side, Surridge held catches which to lesser fieldsmen would not have been chances. He attacked the batsmen, menacing, marauding, unsettling, but all within the laws and spirit of the game.

Tall and sprightly, he bowled his fast-medium to great purpose with unbounded energy and enthusiasm, and he hit a ball with fierce enterprise. There was excitement in the air when Surridge played cricket, and there was a constant sense of urgency that the game must be won as soon as possible. There was joy, but no lack of seriousness, and Jim Laker, at the height of his powers, was once omitted from the side for what his captain considered a breach of discipline on the field.

After five years of success Surridge retired, an Alexander with no more worlds to conquer. County cricket has never seen his equal as a leader of men and relentless motivator. It should not be forgotten that those who have tasted the higher triumphs of Test cricket often find it hardest to strive for greater purpose at county level.

At Surrey, Surridge was succeeded by Peter May, who had already

Peter May – England and Surrey.

succeeded Len Hutton as captain of England. May was the leading batsman of his generation, effortless, graceful, powerful, adaptable. A somewhat shy and reticent man, he has held all the leading positions in the game – captain of England, President of MCC, Chairman of the Test selectors. In a sense, it was his misfortune to follow as captain of club and country two men who had enjoyed unending triumph. It tended to diminish his own achievement. As Surrey continued to win, the Championship title was taken for granted; as England enjoyed a period of prosperity, that too was taken as axiomatic.

As a captain, he inclined more to Hutton than to Surridge. There was caution in his approach. Yet he turned aside the advance of West Indies with a relentless destruction of Ramadhin, and although he has always believed that pace was the match-winner, he led England when Laker and Lock enjoyed their greatest triumphs. For one so quiet and courteous and cautious, there was surprising ruthlessness in his captaincy, yet one is left only with a sharp image of the great qualities of batsmanship. Of the personality of leadership, no clearly defined characteristic remains. This, in itself, may be something of a compliment. May's captaincy had the inestimable quality of unobtrusiveness.

In the 16 years immediately following the Second World War, Len Hutton was, by general consent, the best of England captains and Stuart Surridge the best of county captains. They were of violently contrasting backgrounds and personalities. The first was a professional from the north; the second an amateur from the south. It served only to emphasise most clearly that what mattered in leadership was not to be brought about by some artificial social classification which tried to distinguish between those who were paid and those who were 'unpaid' and to accord an elevated status to the latter, but was to be found within the qualities of the man himself.

Social changes had destroyed a tradition which had long since ceased to have meaning. At the end of the 1962 season, the distinction between amateurs and professionals, between gentlemen and players, was abolished. Henceforth, everyone was to be known as a 'cricketer'.

7 The Age of the Professional

Of the nine county captains appointed at the abolition of the professional-amateur distinction, eight were former professionals. Only Colin Drybrough of Middlesex could be said to have come from the amateur ranks. This new breed of captain took over at a time when cricket itself was undergoing radical changes and was being forced to a reappraisal.

After the boom years immediately following the Second World War, interest in the game had waned. Batting seemed to be dominated by pad play, a zest had gone out of the game and it seemed to be meandering aimlessly, following a pattern imposed upon it nearly a century earlier, unable to come to terms with the demands of the time. Enquiry and debate resolved to bring about change in attitudes, and the abolition of the amateur-professional status was only a first step. In 1963 the long awaited knock-out competition came into being with the 60-over Gillette Cup. It was an instant success, immensely popular with the public. One-day cricket, anathema to the purist, was adored by a new generation.

The John Player Sunday League followed in 1969, and the Benson and Hedges Cup three years later. All three limited-over competitions gained wider television coverage than any cricket had enjoyed before. The Gillette Cup and the Benson and Hedges Cup reached their climaxes before packed houses at Lord's in September and July respectively. Crowds flocked to the Sunday League matches, and support in cricket became partisan.

Where once 17 counties had competed for one trophy which more than a dozen of them knew that they had little or no hope of winning, there were now four competitions, and counties like Essex, Leicestershire, Northamptonshire, Somerset, Sussex and Worcestershire, trophy-less before 1963, dreamed of snatching one of them. So did their supporters. Where once people had gone to the second day of a game little concerned about its eventual outcome and interested only in the cricket, there was now a passionate desire to win, and the responsibility thrust upon county captains was comparable to that borne by football club managers. Cricket had outgrown the leisured calm of its Edwardian days and was now a professional concern backed by sponsors and favoured for business entertaining. Although it was not always to get them, it needed professional managers on and off the field.

Yorkshire, so long at the forefront, were among the first to realise this. They had appointed a professional captain, Vic Wilson, in 1960, and he was succeeded by a cricketer whose approach to the game was always totally and uncompromisingly professional, Brian Close.

Brian Close will remain a cricketer and a captain who excites controversy and debate. In his first year as a Yorkshire player, 1949, 18 years old, Close had been awarded his county cap, completed the 'double' and played for England against New Zealand. His subsequent career never quite lived up to the sensational beginning. His off-breaks and medium pace did not become lethal, his left-handed batting hovered between extremes and his appearances for England were irregular, invariably at time of crisis.

He was an automatic choice as Yorkshire's captain in 1963, for he was the senior professional with 13 years of first-class cricket behind him. He had been a wayward youth, not always receptive to advice, but his knowledge of the game was sound, his tactical sense good. He was a supremely confident man, and he responded eagerly to the responsibilities of leadership.

Under his captaincy, Yorkshire retained the title that they had won in 1962, and they won the Championship again in 1966, 1967 and 1968. In 1965, Close also led his side to victory in the Gillette Cup, so that only in 1964, when they were fifth in the Championship, did Yorkshire fail to win a trophy in Close's first six years of leadership.

In 1963, he had earned one of his recalls to the England side and played a memorable innings of 70, charging down the wicket to the fast bowling of Hall and Griffith, in the dramatic drawn Test at Lord's which ended with England six runs short of their target with their last pair together, one of them Colin Cowdrey, who had broken his arm earlier in the match. Close's dancing down the wicket to Hall and Griffith, which he defended as the only possible counter to the West Indies' slow over-rate, was symptomatic of his positive, aggressive approach to the game. It was not the aggression of the entertaining big hitter, but of the man who attacked in all three departments of the game.

He fielded perilously close to the bat, surviving blows that would have felled an ox. He fielded a yard or two closer to the bat than sense or duty demanded, but he took some unbelievable catches and menaced batsmen in such a way as to give his bowlers a dimension which, in truth, they did not possess.

The legend attendant on his fielding was of his being hit a fearful blow on the head so that his side looked in horror, expecting the skipper to succumb at any second, only to hear him shout 'Catch it!' as the ball bounded some ten yards from his head.

The hardness became the man, and it tended to obscure the calculating, thoughtful aspects of his leadership. Yet how is one to judge a captain's contribution to his side's success? Close's first game as captain of England is a case in point.

In 1966, England suffered indignity at the hands of the West Indies. Relief came only in the second Test at Lord's. The first, third and fourth Tests were lost, two of them by an innings. M.J.K. Smith had led in the first Test, Colin Cowdrey in the next three. The fifth Test match saw Murray replace Parks, John Edrich replace Milburn, Illingworth and Amiss come into the side, and Close supersede Cowdrey. Close had been widely supported in the press who saw him as some northerner in tough, dented armour ready to save an England which had been led astray by flabby southern captaincy.

In fact, England did win by an innings, but quite how much Close had to do with it is hard to assess. Sobers won the toss. Close handled his bowling well and placed his field meaningfully, but in this respect Cowdrey had made no tactical errors. Kanhai hit a hundred and West Indies made 268. Batting number seven, Close wandered out of his ground and was run out by Sobers from silly mid-off for 4. At 166 for 7, England again looked doomed.

Tom Graveney and John Murray added a record 217 for the eighth wicket. Murray proved to those who had left him so long in the cold that he was not only the best wicket-keeper in the country, but a better batsman than most. Both he and Graveney hit centuries. Higgs made 63 and Snow 59 not out. England reached 527, bowled out West Indies for 225 and Close was a hero, even though his contribution to the victory had been hard to gauge except, one presumes, in terms of keeping up morale.

He captained England throughout the following summer, against India and Pakistan, winning both series. He also led Yorkshire to the Championship, but amid anger and controversy.

The trouble arose in the match with Warwickshire at Edgbaston. The home side led by four on the first innings and, in gloomy, showery weather, bowled Yorkshire out for 145 in the second innings on the last day. Warwickshire needed 142 to win in 100 minutes.

From the start, Yorkshire made no secret of their delaying tactics. Defensive fields were set. Bowlers laboured through their overs. Fielders walked slowly to their places. Amiss and Jameson hit lustily to keep Warwickshire abreast of the clock, but the tardiness in Yorkshire's approach to the game frustrated spectators, Warwickshire and the umpires, Charlie Elliott and Laurie Gray.

With 15 minutes remaining and 24 runs needed, Yorkshire appealed against the drizzle. The appeal was rejected, but when the rain became heavier they left the field and were back in the dressing-room before umpires and batsmen had reached the pavilion gate. The rain stopped suddenly and the umpires immediately returned to the middle. Only two more overs were bowled. Trueman bowled one which contained three bouncers, two no-balls and the wicket of Amiss. The other was bowled by Richard Hutton, called slowly from the deep field for the purpose, who also took a wicket. The game was over with Warwickshire nine short of their target.

In the 100 minutes, Yorkshire had bowled only 24 overs, and in the last 15 minutes, as we have noted, two. The hostility to the Yorkshire players as they left the field was intense. The umpires sent in a report which resulted in the Yorkshire committee admitting that Close had adopted delaying tactics and reprimanded him. Legislation was later brought in to ensure that 20 overs were bowled in the last hour, but in the meantime Yorkshire had earned two points for avoiding defeat and went to the top of the Championship which they eventually won.

For Close, the incident came at the wrong time. It is almost certain that he had already been chosen to captain England in the West Indies, but, following the Edgbaston affair, Cowdrey, not Close, was named as skipper. Close did not captain England again although he was recalled to the Test side nine years later when his courage was again needed.

One can understand the selectors' decision to dispense with Close as captain. If an incident like that at Edgbaston occurred in the West Indies, the reaction might be too frightening to consider, to say nothing of the diplomatic repercussions, although one feels that Close would have been appreciated and understood in the Caribbean.

The press was split on the Close-Cowdrey issue. Michael Parkinson, in colourful and humorous manner, suggested that, without Close and under Cowdrey, England had no chance. It was, he argued, a reassertion of Gentlemen and Players. In the event, England won the series by one Test to nil, four being drawn. England have not won a series in the West Indies since.

Three years after being sacked from the England captaincy, Brian Close was dismissed by Yorkshire. It was an astounding decision and one which began a long and bitter struggle within the County which has yet to be fully resolved. The most common explanation for Close's dismissal was his apparent contempt for the limited-over game, but he helped to kindle Somerset's interest for that type of cricket when he captained them from 1972 to 1977.

Even his West Country days were not without controversy. He introduced young Ian Botham and he ordered off A.A. Jones for slackness in the field. Jones moved to Middlesex and helped them to win the Championship.

Close's initial success with Yorkshire confirmed the opinion that to prosper in an increasingly commercial game a county needed a captain who was hard and professional – a Jardine rather than a Chapman. Where amateurs, like Freddie Brown at Northants and Charles Palmer at Leicestershire, had once been imported to lead counties, hardened professionals were now sought to do the same job.

Following his distinguished career with Surrey and England, Tony Lock had emigrated to Australia where he had captained Western Australia when they won the Sheffield Shield, broken the state bowling record and rejuvenated the side to such an extent that his period in charge is still spoken of with reverence. In 1965, he was persuaded to return to England and to play for Leicestershire, and his presence had an immediate effect. In his second season with the Midland county, he took over the captaincy from Hallam who was quite happy to relinquish it.

Lock infected his team with his own exuberance. He was dynamic in the field and urgent in his approach to the game. He had learned much from Surridge and Surrey's golden days, but he was essentially his own man. Leicestershire immediately climbed eight places in the table, and in 1967, they finished joint second in the Championship, the highest position that they had ever attained. Lock's drive and brilliance in the field were apparent for all to see, as was the Leicestershire players' response to their captain. Suddenly, and unexpectedly, after two years in which Leicestershire cricket had thrived, Lock decided not to return to England, and the brief love affair was over.

Hallam hastily took over the captaincy, but in 1969, with troubles brewing at Yorkshire, Ray Illingworth left his native county and came to Leicestershire as captain. He had had 18 seasons in first-class cricket, was a highly successful county all-rounder and had played often for England without ever really suggesting a permanent place in the Test side. As an off-break bowler he could not really be classed better than Titmus, but he was an intelligent bowler with a classic delivery, while his batting was solid, determined and resolute. Above all, he was a fearless and formidable opponent and a captain whose men supported him as loyally and fully as he supported them. A team

Ray Illingworth.

under Illingworth's leadership was at once tight-knit, jealous of honour.

He led Leicestershire for ten years, 1969 to 1978, and during that time they won the Championship for the first time, 1975, took the John Player League in 1974 and 1977, and won the Benson and

Hedges Cup in 1972 and 1975. His impact on his new county was immediate, and they were pressing hard for the Championship in the early days of his rule, but an injury to Colin Cowdrey thrust Illingworth into the captaincy of England after only twelve matches as captain of Leicestershire. England beat the West Indies by ten wickets, took the three-Test series and Illingworth's reign as captain of his country had begun in triumph. It was to continue in the same vein.

He was a tough leader and a shrewd tactician. He led England in 31 Tests and among his victories was the series in Australia, 1970–71, a feat which only Chapman, Jardine and Hutton had achieved since the First World War. His term as England's captain came to an end in 1973 when his side received a mauling at the hands of West Indies at Lord's, the 'bomb scare' Test.

Illingworth was meticulous and totally professional in everything he did in the game. One emphasises again the term professional because Illingworth, like Brearley after him, was committed to the ideal that his men should gain due reward and benefit from the game. He saw this as a vital means of achieving unity, and his men responded to it. He was eminently popular.

Close and Illingworth, as England captains, were, in effect, belated appointments, for, in spite of the abolition of the distinction between cricketers in 1963, the leaders after Hutton were all from the 'amateur' stable – May, Cowdrey, Dexter, and M.J.K. Smith – yet at county level it was generally the experienced professional who was becoming dominant.

Don Kenyon led Worcestershire with intelligence and sensitivity from 1959 to 1967, during which time the County won the Championship for the first time and were twice finalists in the Gillette Cup. He was succeeded in turn by Tom Graveney and Norman Gifford, yet these three appointments were, in a sense, automatic. The same could not be said of appointments made by Lancashire and Essex.

When Trevor Bailey retired at the end of the 1966 season Essex suprised many people, including some of their own supporters, by naming Brian Taylor as captain. Barry Knight, the England all-rounder, left Essex in protest and later qualified for Leicestershire. The staff was reduced to twelve, for Essex were in grave financial trouble at the time, and Taylor was asked to manage within extreme limitations.

Taylor's career had not developed as some had prophesied. He had been seen as a wicket-keeper capable of succeeding Godfrey Evans and as a left-handed batsman who could wallop a ball consistently hard. He had never quite blossomed into the cricketer that had been expected, but he was a rich and forceful character, and Essex saw him as the man capable of leading them from a possession of economic crisis and moderate playing performance.

Taylor was neither a great tactician nor a great thinker on the game. His qualities lay in other directions, and they were qualities admirably suited to leading a small squad of untried and mainly untested young men. He was a strong disciplinarian, a fitness fanatic, and passionately devoted to the well-being of those whom he commanded. A man of the utmost integrity, one who radiated honest endeavour, he was not an officer, but he was a remarkable sergeant-major.

The record books will show that Essex won nothing under Taylor, yet he transformed his county into a side with professional standards, in dress, in fitness, in fielding, in commitment, in running between the wickets. He repaired morale and fostered aggression, and although he was unlucky not to lead his side to a trophy, he set the foundation on which future triumphs were built, and brought his team to a state of physical application comparable to that of a professional football side. Such a thing had not been known before, nor could it have been achieved when the captain was an amateur in many cases remote from his side, socially and physically.

If Taylor had been a surprise choice at Essex, a year later, at Old Trafford, Jack Bond was an even more astonishing appointment. Bond had first played for Lancashire in 1955, but had failed to establish himself as a batsman in a side which was undergoing one of the unhappiest periods in its history.

We have traced events following the dismissal of Fallows and the sad reign of Bob Barber. Lancashire cricket remained in the doldrums. Neither Grieves nor Statham could revive a side from which the zest had gone and which was troubled by conflict and dissension behind the scenes. There were several fine players on the staff, but far too many were consistently playing below their capabilities.

A shake-up on the committee saw Cedric Rhoades emerge as Chairman. A man of energy and passion for Lancashire cricket, he determined that Lancashire cricket would be put back to its position of former glory. Jack Bond was appointed captain to carry out this task.

Bond had proved very successful as captain of the second eleven, for he possessed that magical quality of being able to get the best out of his men. Backed by chairman and committee, Bond brushed away the apathy from Old Trafford and a new dawn beckoned for Lancashire cricket. Bond led his side to the John Player League title in its inaugural season, 1969, drove them to third place in the Championship in 1970 when they retained the John Player League and won the Gillette Cup. They were to dominate one-day cricket by winning the 60-over competition three years in succession, the last, 1972, being the final year of Bond's leadership.

Crowds poured back to Old Trafford. When Lancashire beat Yorkshire in August 1970 to clinch the Sunday league title, 28,000 people were present. A year later, in the semi-final of the Gillette Cup, a capacity crowd, with thousands locked out before play began, were kept until nine o'clock when, in near darkness, Lancashire beat Gloucestershire in one of the most dramatic finishes ever seen in a cricket match. Hughes was the hero of that game, hitting Mortimore for 24 in one over, but it was Bond who had stayed at a crucial time and who made the winning hit in the over after Hughes's onslaught.

In the final, against Kent, Asif Iqbal, with a brilliant innings of 89 to follow his fine bowling, appeared to be taking his side to a comfortable victory; but he drove Simmons wide of extra-cover, hard and cleanly, where Bond suddenly took off and plucked the ball out of the air and clutched it as he rolled over and over on the ground. Lancashire went on to win the game by 24 runs. With such breath-taking catches and brilliant fielding, Bond was a constant source of inspiration to his side and a demoraliser of the opposition.

Under his leadership, Lancashire became a great attraction, drawing vast crowds to grounds wherever they played in one-day matches. In their heyday, they reached a status in cricket comparable to that of Liverpool, Manchester United or Arsenal in football.

Bond was modest and quietly assertive. He instructed his men always to go out and enjoy themselves, and they did, and so did those who watched them. He was sensitive, tactful and listened to grievances and encouraged debate. Ultimately he made the decisions, but he had achieved a sense of integration. He believed in Lancashire and in its players, and he encouraged them to belief in themselves which many had lacked until his time.

His later career, an unwise period at Trent Bridge and a return to Old Trafford as manager, a move that was not greatly successful, should not obscure the fact that he proved at county level that the honest professional, strong in the traditions of the game which he knew well and honoured deeply, was at least on a par as a captain with some of the great amateur leaders of the past like Green, Sellers and Robins.

In 1963, legislation had wiped out the distinction that existed between amateur and professional. By 1973, the achievements of Illingworth, Bond and the rest had made it seem that that distinction had never existed.

8 Prophets from Afar

We have tended to concentrate our attention on cricket in England where captaincy has been seen as an issue separate from that of choosing the rest of the side. We have shown how, at both Test and county level, captains were appointed who were not necessarily worth their place in the side on playing ability. In contrast, in Australia, it was always the custom to choose the eleven best players and find the captain from among them. The Australians, although receiving adequate sums, were always considered to be amateurs when they were touring England. As J.C. Clay, one of the wisest and best of captains with Glamorgan, commented, 'In any case, the only sane view of the amateur or professional question is the Australian one – "Call us what you something well like but we want half the gate."'

The Australian attitude to captaincy echoed this, but in the early days of Test cricket, they were generally noted for poor leadership, and in recent years, their captains have varied greatly in quality.

Bradman has been recognised as outstanding, but he was the world's greatest batsman and commanded a very strong side, particularly in the immediate post-war years. Hassett and Ian Johnson were disappointments, Ian Craig a surprise choice who passed almost unnoticed outside his own country. The Chappell brothers contrasted in approach, but both were effective. Neither Yallop nor Hughes had the happiest of reigns, and Border's path to success in the 1987 World Cup was long and painful. Keith Miller and Rodney Marsh, of different generations, were fine leaders whose aggressive approach was not always appreciated by the authorities. Since Bradman, the one leader of genius to emerge in Australia at Test level was Richie Benaud.

Benaud led a side of moderate ability at top level with an

Richie Benaud revitalised Australian cricket.

intelligence and panache that was able to overcome stronger sides. Calm and authoritative, but always with a sense of fun, he perceived quicker and more deeply than others. There was a wit and vitality in his thinking which made his actions on the cricket field exciting to watch and which, in the days since, have made him an outstanding commentator.

At state level in Australia, three captains have been considered as being head and shoulders above others in recent years, John Inverarity, Tony Lock and Jack Simmons. The last two, of course, were English.

The problems in the choice of captain are probably deeper in India than anywhere else in the world, for the pressures themselves for a leader to bring success are infinitely greater than they are elsewhere.

Wadekar triumphed in England, but was instantly replaced when he failed, and Gavaskar and Kapil Dev, arguably the best two cricketers that India has produced, have only confirmed the belief that the best player does not necessarily make a good captain.

If India's early days in Test cricket were blighted by the need to have a man of esteemed position in authority irrespective of his merits as a cricketer so, to a lesser extent, were those of West Indies. In his *Cricket From the Grandstand*, Keith Miller wrote:

> Another problem in West Indies cricket is that the captain has usually been chosen from among the European stock. Just think of the most famous West Indies cricketers . . . Learie Constantine, George Headley, Frank Worrell, Everton Weekes, Clyde Walcott . . . all are coloured, but none has led his country. Yet Worrell was often skipper of Commonwealth tours in India, and he did a fine job.

After this was written Worrell did become captain of West Indies and led them to heights never before attained, but C.L.R. James, the West Indian cricket writer, philosopher and political thinker, supported Miller's view. He reported a conversation with Clyde Walcott:

> One evening in British Guiana we were talking about captaincy. Suddenly Clyde, who is always circumspect in his speech, blurted out: 'You know who will be captain in England in 1963? You see that Barbados boy, Bynoe, who went to India? He has only to make fifty in one innings and he will be the captain.'
>
> Bynoe is white.

In the event, Frank Worrell was made captain, West Indies won the series 3–1 and began one of the great periods in their cricket.

One mentions these points to show that the problem of social distinction which had plagued English cricket in its appointment of captains was suffered elsewhere in the world. Yet in some ways the erosion of this distinction brought with it other problems. Whereas clubs had known exactly where to find a captain and in early days, as with Jewell at Worcestershire, the Walkers at Middlesex, Green at Essex and the Hill-Woods at Derbyshire, had relied upon the chosen man for financial survival, a point which should never be forgotten, they were now confronted with deciding exactly what qualities they were looking for in a leader. In this respect, it is interesting to note that two of the three most noted Sheffield Shield captains who we have mentioned have been importations, Lock and Simmons.

The feeling that someone from outside can better fit a position of authority and command than someone in residence is not restricted to cricket. In business and commerce, managers and directors are brought in from other firms, and in education, heads and deputies are invariably chosen from those in lesser positions in other establishments. There is a belief that they will bring with them some magic powers that will cure all the ills. County cricket clubs, like many other organisations, look for messiahs.

Brian Bolus never captained his own county, Yorkshire, but he led both Derbyshire and Nottinghamshire. Leicestershire imported Watson, Lock and Illingworth, all with marked success. Close moved to Somerset; Gifford eventually took over at Warwickshire. The county seemingly in perpetual search for an external miracle was Glamorgan.

Captained from 1947 to 1960 by the fiery Wilf Wooller, a firm believer in traditional values and order, Glamorgan appointed Ossie Wheatley from Warwickshire as his successor, and he, in turn, was succeeded by Tony Lewis, another university man, albeit a Welshman. All three were good leaders in different styles, and Lewis was particularly effective and popular. He was most unlucky not to play for England before captaining the side to India and Pakistan in 1972–73, for, in many ways, the chance came too late for him. He proved to be a great success, and his popularity from that tour has not diminished on the Indian sub-continent, nor among those who travelled with him.

Lewis was a good batsman and a lively personality, sensitive to the social needs of the game and to its heritage. Injury forced him to leave cricket shortly after that tour, and he was replaced as Glamorgan skipper by Majid J. Khan, the brilliant Pakistani player, whom Glamorgan had registered as their overseas player in 1968. Under Lewis, Glamorgan cricket had been buoyant. They won the Championship in 1969 and finished third and second each side of that triumph. They had slipped down the table in 1971, and the decline continued under Majid Khan.

Lewis's account of the events are revealing and symptomatic of what was happening elsewhere at the time. He recognised

> the growing ferment among professional cricketers all over the country. For years the cricketer had been underpaid. Top county salaries were around the £2,000 a year mark. Yet more and more cricket was being covered by television which attracted new sponsorship. How much of that cash was coming to the players? Not enough, that was certain. Clubs said that they needed it and so they did, but they were going to have to change their priorities by the end of the decade, and it took a players' revolution to achieve it.

The revolution of course was the Packer Affair wherein leading players from all over the world were paid large sums in a commercially staged international, but officially unrecognised, venture in Australia. The outcome was that players' salaries were raised, and even more money came into the game, but that was seven years ahead, and Majid, straight from captaincy at Cambridge and a reluctant accepter of the Glamorgan leadership, took over at a time of disaffection and unrest. 'Given time,' says Lewis, 'he might well have been a proper choice, but in 1973, at least in Glamorgan, there was no way in which a 26-year-old Muslim was going to be able to communicate with a dissident and only moderately talented Welsh county side.'

Majid's sad reign ended in 1976 in 'public disarray and private torture'. Allan Jones, the veteran left-handed opener, took over in mid-season, but two and a half years later, with Glamorgan now in an abyss, partly of their own making, he stepped aside as Robin Hobbs, who had retired from Essex disillusioned with first-class cricket four years earlier, was brought in as captain.

It was the popular pattern, the messiah from a distant land who would bring salvation. Hobbs lasted only a year as captain, and local hero Malcolm Nash became captain, but in 1983, Mike Selvey was imported from Middlesex. He lasted longer, but was no more successful than Hobbs. Ontong followed, only to resign in mid-season and to be replaced by Hugh Morris, a young man with a hard task. At last Glamorgan began some sensible rebuilding on a firmer basis.

One of the first counties to introduce a cricketer from outside in expectation that he would right their wrongs was Nottinghamshire, who were primarily responsible for the legislation which allowed counties immediate registration of an overseas player in 1968. They, seemingly, had the prize capture when their immediate registration was Gary Sobers, unquestionably the greatest cricketer in the world at the time.

Sobers was immediately appointed captain. Membership and gate receipts increased at Trent Bridge, and Sobers produced some memorably entertaining moments, but his leadership at Test and county level was never of the highest calibre, perhaps because he was too good a natural player to be a deep-thinking, tactically minded captain. The impetus of his arrival took Notts to fourth in the Championship, but they fell away again, and the years under Sobers brought no trophies, the winning of which was now demanded by followers of the game. As counties searched for them, blame was apportioned and heads rolled.

Derbyshire, in particular, struggled through the 1970s. From 1971 to 1976, they did not escape the bottom three in the County Championship. Leadership proved to be a most difficult problem. Buxton gave way to Bolus, who resigned in mid-season in 1975 to hand over to Bob Taylor. There is no more likeable person in cricket than Taylor, but he found that combining the job of wicket-keeper with that of captain was impossible, and he stood aside in the middle of the 1976 season when Eddie Barlow took over.

The South African all-rounder was in his first season with the county. There was no immediate material reward from Barlow's accession to the captaincy, but his second season, his first full season as captain, brought a marked improvement.

A medium-pace bowler, pugnacious batsman and a tigerish fieldsman, Barlow came to Derbyshire with the experience of 30 Test matches behind him. The tenacious qualities which permeated Barlow's cricket were the qualities which Derbyshire most lacked, and his captaincy transformed the county. He spent hours working in the nets with players like Miller, who has had so much talent which has been so rarely used, and Hill, and he renewed the confidence of the side. In 1977, Derbyshire leapt up the table, and the following year, which was to be Barlow's last, they reached the final of the Benson and Hedges Cup.

Michael Carey, based in Derby and writing for *Wisden*, had no doubt as to the reason for Derbyshire's revival. He gave total credit to Barlow's leadership. 'He welded what had been a collection of individuals into a team, starting with a winter fitness programme which produced not only stamina but discipline and self-confidence and, therefore, greater quality and consistency throughout the team.'

Barlow decided that three years in county cricket was enough, and his departure again created a captaincy crisis at Derbyshire. David Steele, imported from Northants, found the job not to his liking and resigned after half a season before returning to his original county.

Gary Sobers reflects. He was one of the greatest cricketers the world has known, but his captaincy was of doubtful quality.

Barry Wood surrendered the captaincy of Derbyshire and left the county in acrimony.

Geoff Miller took over, but he, too, left in mid-season to be replaced by Barry Wood.

Wood was another importation, this time from Lancashire, but his reign, initially successful, ended in some acrimony. He had taken over from Miller midway through the 1981 season. Now, in the first week of May 1983, he stated that he found captaincy too demanding, for it was affecting his form as an opening batsman and bowler. The Derbyshire committee took the brave step of appointing 22-year-old Kim Barnett in his place, and the result was that Derbyshire won more games than they had won since Derek Morgan had been captain in 1966.

Wood was left out of the side at the beginning of June, and his response was to say that his omission was an insult. He later refused to give support to captain or administration, and his playing days, never totally harmonious, were over. His resignation had meant that for the fifth time in nine years Derbyshire had been forced to make a change of captaincy during the season.

Thankfully for Derbyshire cricket, Kim Barnett has remained in control ever since and the county has begun to establish a presence in all competitions.

Derbyshire were not alone in turning to an overseas player in their search for a captain. Sobers at Nottinghamshire we have already mentioned, while Northants turned to Mushtaq Mohammad and Gloucestershire were led by Mike Procter.

The fortunes of the western county had been revived under Tony Brown, but he stepped down in 1977 and Procter, one of the world's greatest all-rounders whose appearances in Test cricket had been limited because of South Africa's exclusion from the international arena, took over. Leaders fall into two categories: those who manipulate and control with intellectual clarity while not necessarily being great performers; and those who inspire by example. Procter fell into the second category.

He was not an unthinking cricketer, but he led from the front. For Gloucestershire, he was the greatest match-winner since W.G. Grace. With the bat, with the ball or in the field, he was always contributing something. He was an entertainer of the highest quality, and crowds thrilled to him. Fellow players marvelled at him and responded to his inspiration, but he could be a hard task master. As one of his team was to say later, 'The trouble with Prockie was that he was so good that he thought everyone else should be the same. He was always doing something, hitting a six, bowling people out, taking a wonderful catch, and if you didn't take a wicket, put down a catch or couldn't score a run, he thought that you weren't trying.'

Procter's value to Gloucestershire as player and captain was immense. He threw himself totally into the West Country cause. There was never a sense that he was an outsider. He merged, mixed and was absorbed as if his birth-place had been Cheltenham and his school-days spent in Stroud. His complete identification with the county was one of the finest qualities of his leadership.

Barlow had worked miracles at Derbyshire. Procter had breathed life into Gloucestershire. Northants had won the Gillette Cup, the first trophy in their history, under Mushtaq Mohammad. A pattern had clearly emerged. The success that had become all important to counties was more likely to be achieved under the captaincy of a noted cricketer who had been imported for that purpose. It was an imitation

Mike Procter – an imported inspiration for Gloucestershire.

of the practice prevalent in industry and commerce. The trouble was that, by the end of the 1970s with Brearley having announced his retirement from Test cricket, England faced a crisis of captaincy. The Test and County Cricket Board recognised the problem and issued a statement in 1980 asking that counties should only appoint English-born players as captain. The plea was ignored. Counties were concerned with their own immediate financial problems for which trophy-winning was the balm, rather than with the wider implications of Test cricket from which, however, they drew a large proportion of their incomes.

Kent chose Asif Iqbal of Pakistan, Lancashire opted for Clive Lloyd and Worcestershire elected Glenn Turner. With Clive Rice at Notts and Procter at Gloucestershire already in command, five of the 17 counties in 1981 were led by overseas players.

The three new appointments were all made in an attempt to lift flagging fortunes. Worcestershire had dispensed with Norman Gifford, who was at the veteran stage, but who was subsequently to move to Warwickshire where he became captain until the end of the 1987 season. New Zealander Glenn Turner was in the position of senior professional at Worcestershire and was a natural successor to Gifford.

Clive Lloyd was already established as captain of West Indies who were dominant in world cricket, and Lancashire were again undergoing one of the less happy periods, having found it difficult to replace Bond, with neither David Lloyd nor Frank Hayes enjoying the happiest of times. Lloyd's qualities as a captain remain rather vague. Some have said that his appointment at Old Trafford in 1981 came too late. He was to remain until 1983, and was then reappointed for one more season in 1986. But triumphant as West Indies were under his leadership, he never impressed as a great tactician, neither as a County nor as a Test captain, and was certainly not a strong disciplinarian. Indeed, if a captain earns plaudits for his side's successes, so must he take the criticism for some of their failings. Clive Lloyd was captain of West Indies at a time when Test cricket produced some of its most unsavoury incidents in terms of deliberate short-pitched bowling and contempt for the rulings of umpires.

Like Lloyd at Old Trafford, Asif Iqbal at Kent was appointed to try to lift an ailing side. The traumas that had attended Kent cricket in the 1950s had been forgotten during the 14 years of Colin Cowdrey's reign as captain. Under Cowdrey, Kent had won the Championship and the Gillette Cup, and they enjoyed a golden period under his successor, Mike Denness.

Denness believed that the side at his disposal was best equipped to prosper in limited-over cricket, and prosper they did. Denness was captain of Kent from 1972 to 1976 and during that time they won the Gillette Cup, the Benson and Hedges Cup and three times the John Player Sunday League.

Like Colin Cowdrey, Mike Denness was not too well treated at Test level. Cowdrey had been seen as May's automatic successor. Just as May had served as lieutenant under Hutton and had inherited much of the Yorkshireman's steeliness, so Cowdrey followed May in style while stamping his own brand of homely warmth on the job.

When May fell ill in the West Indies, 1959–60, Cowdrey took over. He continued as captain against South Africa and for the first two Tests against Australia in 1961, after which May resumed with Cowdrey again his lieutenant. With neither May nor Cowdrey available, Ted Dexter led England in India and Pakistan in 1961–62.

In 1962, when Pakistan were the visitors to England, the selectors decided that Cowdrey and Dexter would vie for the position of England captain. Dexter led in the first two Tests, both of which England won easily. Cowdrey was captain for the third Test which England won by an innings and 117 runs. One cannot think that the England side could have been better led. Batsmen's weaknesses were exploited. Trueman and Titmus were intelligently used, and Pakistan's limitations were most cruelly exposed. It did not matter. Dexter was named as captain of the side to go to Australia.

Sussex enjoyed some success in limited-over cricket under Dexter's guidance, but he is not remembered as one of the best of captains at county or Test level. An extravagantly gifted and hugely entertaining batsman, Ted Dexter was perhaps too talented in too many directions to make an ideal captain. The game seemed to bore him too easily. He had a detachment that Brearley was to use to great effect, but in Dexter's case it served only to distance him from his men. His judgment of a player was not always sound, and it was wrong assessments, such as in the choice of wicket-keepers, that created a lack of confidence in him. For a man of such exuberant an approach to batting and with the love of a wager, his captaincy was surprisingly conservative. The series in Australia, 1962–63, was drawn, one Test each, and Dexter himself scored 481 runs, a record by an England captain in Australia, but there was some surprisingly dull cricket played on both sides. Paradoxically, since his retirement, Dexter has proved to be one of the great thinkers on the game. His counsel is wise, his advice sought by many.

The following year, Cowdrey had his arm broken in the Lord's Test match against West Indies. Mike Smith now moved up to take England to India, and then to South Africa in 1964–65. Now Cowdrey was Smith's second-in-command until, in 1966, he was again England's captain, against the strong West Indies side. This was the series in which Close took over for the final Test, when Cowdrey was dropped after England had lost three of the first four Tests.

The recall came after Close's misdemeanour, and victory in the West Indies followed. Cowdrey was a hero, and he took England to a drawn series with Australia in 1968, although he himself missed the fourth Test through injury. On a rain-affected wicket, he used Underwood to undermine the Australian batting at The Oval after he had organised a band of volunteers in mopping up operations on the last day to make play possible.

He nursed England through riots in Pakistan and was preparing to meet West Indies in 1969 when, on Sunday 25 May, he tore an Achilles tendon while batting in a John Player League match. Ray Illingworth replaced him. It was the cruellest of injuries, and, in effect, it brought an end to Cowdrey's career as England captain. Illingworth was chosen to take England to Australia in 1970–71, with Cowdrey, bitterly disappointed, a reluctant vice-captain yet again.

Mike Denness's reign was briefer and equally unlucky. He first played for England, against New Zealand, at The Oval in 1969. When Tony Lewis took the England side to India and Pakistan in 1972–73 he appointed Denness as vice-captain. Lewis's original intention was to make Geoff Boycott vice-captain, but Boycott declined to make the tour.

The next time Denness appeared in an England side was the following winter when he was captain of the side that went to the Caribbean. England gained a creditable draw in the series, but the tour was to have repercussions. Boycott, after one more Test, against India in 1974, went into voluntary exile, refusing to play Test cricket under Denness or, indeed, under his successor Tony Greig. In his autobiography, Boycott made vitriolic attacks on both men, Denness, in particular, whom he considered to be the worst of Test captains and, as a batsman, not up to international standard. Greig he saw as interested only in his own self-advancement. It was not a happy time.

Denness led England to an emphatic win over India and three draws against Pakistan. Then he took the side to Australia. For Denness, and for England, the series was a disaster. Lillee and Thomson emerged as the most frightening pair of Australian pace bowlers that England had encountered since McDonald and Gregory 54 years earlier. Amiss and Edrich sustained fractured hands in the first Test to weaken a side that had not been one of England's strongest, and Colin Cowdrey was flown out as a replacement, so making his sixth tour of Australia. A shattered England side returned home beaten by four Tests to one. Australia followed England home for the World Cup and a four-match Test series.

Denness won the toss at Edgbaston, put Australia in and lost by an innnings. It was the end for the Kent captain who had led England against two of the strongest post-war Test sides in their own countries. His record as captain gave credence to the old professionals' belief that it is not how you lead that matters, but when and against whom.

Events had taken their toll of Denness. In spite of his six one-day trophy successes, all was not well at Kent where there were changes in administration as well as on the field. He resigned the captaincy and left the Club, moving across the Thames to Essex. Asif Iqbal replaced him for one season before Alan Ealham was appointed.

Ealham was, in one sense, in the Jack Bond tradition, a batsman of average ability, but a fielder of the very highest quality. In his first season as captain, Kent won the Championship and the Benson and Hedges Cup. There were smiles at Canterbury, but they were to disappear quickly. Nothing was won in 1979, and in 1980, Kent slipped to an unacceptable sixteenth in the County Championship, eleventh in the John Player League, their worst position ever, were knocked out in the first round of the Gillette Cup and failed to qualify for the quarter-finals of the Benson and Hedges Cup.

Much blame was laid at Ealham's door. It was questioned as to whether or not he was really worth his place in the side. Two months after the end of the season, he was relieved of the captaincy and, for one year, Asif Iqbal was reinstated. Ealham remained a contracted player for two more seasons, but, in truth, his playing days were effectively at an end.

Tavaré replaced Asif Iqbal; Chris Cowdrey replaced Tavaré. The penalities for failure to win trophies now rested as heavily on the captain of a county cricket team as they did on the manager of a First Division football club.

9 Brearley and Botham

Should any doubt the pressures that captains were under by the end of the 1970s, the demand that the trophy cabinet in the committee room be filled, they need only consider the plight of Somerset. Founded in 1875, they had won nothing in 103 years. Beating Essex in a thrilling Gillette Cup semi-final at Taunton in 1978, they gave a disappointing performance in the final and were well beaten by Sussex. The bitterness of this defeat was increased when they failed also to win the John Player League although they finished level on points with the Champions, Hampshire.

Somerset possessed one of the most attractive sides in the country. They had Viv Richards, perhaps the most exciting batsman that the game had seen since the days of Denis Compton and one who attracted large crowds. They had Joel Garner, the giant West Indian fast bowler. They had Ian Botham, challenging Grace as the greatest all-rounder in cricket history and Jessop as the greatest hitter. They were most ably led by Brian Rose, astute, sensitive and intelligent, and well represented by such consistent cricketers as Roebuck, Marks, Dredge and Taylor. They played entertaining cricket, and they had nothing to show for it.

They were particularly adept at the one-day game, and it was on these competitions that Rose set his sights. The 1979 season began well for them. They got off to a good start in the John Player League and won their first three matches in the zonal round of the Benson and Hedges Cup, beating Gloucestershire, Glamorgan and Minor Counties (South). This meant that they travelled to Worcester for their last match at the top of their group and with best striking rate in the group, one wicket every 32.96 balls.

The match at Worcester was delayed until the second of the days allocated, 24 May. Rose won the toss and, batting first, declared after one over during which Vanburn Holder had conceded one no-ball. A bewildered Worcestershire left the field. Spectators, few in number, were stunned and angry. Somerset bowled ten balls, and from the tenth, Glenn Turner hit the winning run. The game had lasted under a quarter of an hour.

In deliberately losing the match, Rose had preserved Somerset's superior striking rate and thereby ensured that his side would qualify for the quarter-finals. Public reaction was that Rose had sacrificed all known cricketing principles. His response was that his only duty was to Somerset cricket, and that Somerset were most anxious to win.

The cricket world were unsympathetic to this argument, and at a meeting of the TCCB at Lord's on 1 June, Somerset were disqualified from the Benson and Hedges Cup on a vote of 17 to one, Derbyshire being the only county to support them. In the opinion of the majority, Somerset had brought the game into disrepute.

This sorry little episode has been obscured by later events. Somerset went on to win both the John Player League and the Gillette Cup that same season, won the Benson and Hedges Cup in 1981 and 1982 and took the NatWest Trophy in 1983. Their vociferous, clamouring supporters were appeased. The Club itself remained unrepentant over the events at Worcester. Their handbook for the following season made no mention of the Benson and Hedges Cup. It simply pretended that the competition had never taken place. In a sense, Somerset were more honest than others. They had demonstrated openly that cricket was now about winning and nothing else. Winning also now brought great financial rewards.

Brian Rose was a good captain. He had trained at Borough Road College, Isleworth, noted for excellence in sport, and he was an experienced and dedicated professional who had made his début at the age of 19 and learned the game the hard way through years of endeavour and frustration. He led Somerset in their best years, and one cannot help but feel that when he stepped aside at the end of the 1983 season it was due to some pressure from higher authority who still saw Botham as an England captain and wanted him practised in the art of leadership. By then, in fact, Botham's span as captain of England was over.

Ian Botham's Test career began in 1977, a fortuitous time. The Centenary Test in Melbourne three months earlier had marked the end of Tony Greig's career as England captain. A man of great panache, though no tactical genius, Greig had been revealed as the master agent behind the Packer revolution, using his position as England captain to aid him in his recruitment of some of the world's leading players as members of Kerry Packer's World Series Cricket

Tony Greig.

organisation. Greig was stripped of the England captaincy although his successor, Mike Brearley, insisted that he should remain in the side.

The 1977 series was to see the end of Greig's Test career. He did not return to cricket in England after his final involvement with the Packer international series in Australia. His departure left a space for an all-rounder in the England side which Botham filled more than adequately.

The Packer interlude was to bring financial reward to all cricketers. Pay structures were revised, sponsorship deals increased and those, like Botham, Brearley, Gooch and Gower whose Test careers were mainly in the post-Packer period, became richer men than those whose Test appearances pre-dated 1978.

It is often forgotten that Mike Brearley had already won a place in the England side before he was made captain, which, as a few years earlier he had seemed lost to the game, was remarkable.

Brearley's record at Cambridge had been outstanding. He won his blue in all four years, 1961 to 1964, and was the captain of the side in his last two years. Returning to the University in 1968 for research, although not qualified for the Varsity match, he brought his total number of runs for Cambridge to a record 4,310. His academic record surpassed his sporting record. He took a first in Classics and an upper second in Moral Sciences and was absent from cricket in England in 1966 and 1967 while pursuing his studies in the United States.

Middlesex and England had been excited by his cricketing promise while at Cambridge, but he had a disastrous tour of South Africa, 1964–65, and although capped by Middlesex in 1964, he did not score a championship century until 1973. His appearances were infrequent, and from 1968 to 1970, they were little more than half a season. Yet, in 1971, Middlesex appointed him captain.

The announcement was not unexpected, for it was apparent that Middlesex had lured him back to first-class cricket with promise of the captaincy. He had led MCC Under-25 team in Pakistan in 1966–67, had scored heavily, averaging 132.16, and had impressed as a leader. His appointment as captain of Middlesex, however, was greeted with general dismay. Brearley's background, City of London School, University of Cambridge, was so obviously 'amateur'. He was replacing two top professionals, Titmus and Parfitt, although neither had made a very good job of captaincy.

Middlesex had always been strong in the amateur tradition. Even after the abolition of the demarcation between amateur and professional, they had gone for Drybrough as captain, maintaining old ideas. Yet they could argue that under Titmus and then Parfitt, they had played some of the least enterprising cricket in their history although they had a highly talented side. Indeed, a notorious match against Hampshire at Lord's in 1967 when, over three days, not even first innings points were decided, marked a dreadful low point.

The selection of Brearley as captain was controversial, but it proved to be inspired. He inherited a talented but disunited Middlesex side and reshaped it. There was no instant success, but there was a more positive approach to cricket at Lord's. In 1975, Middlesex reached the finals of the Benson and Hedges Cup and the Gillette Cup. They won the Championship in 1976 and 1977 when they also took the Gillette Cup. There was another Championship in 1980 and again in 1982, Brearley's last year, and the NatWest Trophy in 1980. Only Essex could challenge Middlesex's record during the period.

Playing mostly as an opener, Brearley began to score consistently. Originally a wicket-keeper, he now excelled at slip. In 1976, with Boycott in his self-imposed exile and England struggling to find an opening batsman capable of dealing with the West Indian pace men, Brearley was called up for the first two Test matches. He scored 0, 17, 40 and 13, and he failed to convince people that he was a Test cricketer. As a batsman, he was never to prove himself a Test player.

His 39 Tests brought him only 1,442 runs, average 22.88, yet over the next few years he was the first choice for the England side.

As Middlesex had won the Championship under his leadership, he was named as Greig's vice-captain for the tour of India, 1976–77. This was hard on David Steele who had batted bravely against West Indies and found himself without a place on the trip to India. Brearley played in all five Tests and hit 91, his highest Test score, in the last match of the series. He also played in the Centenary Test in Melbourne, by which time the seeds of the Packer rebellion had been sown.

When the Australians came to England in 1977 Brearley took over as captain from the disgraced Greig. It was a series of romance. Botham made his sensational entry into Test cricket with five wickets at Trent Bridge, Boycott ended his exile and hit his hundredth hundred at Headingley, and England resoundingly regained the 'Ashes' by three matches to nil against a dispirited and disunited Australian side.

Brearley now led England to Pakistan and New Zealand. A weak and inexperienced England side did not find life easy, particularly after Brearley had his arm broken in a one-day match shortly before the third Test in Pakistan. Boycott took over and was captain of England when New Zealand won for the first time.

Boycott's reign as captain of his country was to be brief and no happier nor any more successful than his captaincy of his county. He was a cricketer blinkered by his own performances, too introspective, too complex and too vulnerable as a person to succeed as a leader.

Brearley was back in time to lead England against Pakistan, much decimated by the Packer circus, and New Zealand in the summer of 1978. Both countries were swept aside, as was Australia the following winter.

Australia had been totally ravaged by the Packer affair, and an England side bubbling with enthusiasm routed a team which was scarcely of Test standard by five Tests to one. Brearley had led England to ten wins and five draws before that defeat at Melbourne on 3 January 1979, and he had the comfort of knowing that no side had ever before gained five victories in a rubber in Australia, save Australia themselves.

The second World Cup in England in 1979 saw England play some inspiring cricket on their way to the final where for much of the time they looked to have the better of the West Indies. In the end, England lost, mainly due to some faulty selection and the genius of Richards, supported by Collis King. Brearley led England to another victory in the series against India which followed the World Cup.

Peace with Packer had now been achieved, and the Australian

Board of Control, desperate to repair the financial and morale-sapping damage that had been done, begged England to send a team to Australia in the winter of 1979–80. Reluctantly, the TCCB agreed. Brearley's men, confronted by an Australian side that was at full strength for the first time in over three years, lost all three Tests. The series was hastily arranged and should not have been played, but one was left with the feeling that England had been living in a dream world since 1977.

Victory in the Jubilee Test in Bombay on the way back to England was to have marked the end of Brearley's international career. He had intended that 1979 should be his last year in Test cricket. His retirement left a void, and one which brought the unheeded TCCB appeal that counties should appoint only English-born players as county captains.

In business, it is believed that it is the first duty of a managing director to find his successor. Whether this is possible in cricket is doubtful, nor can we ever be sure whom Brearley recommended, if anybody. Although they tried to hide the fact later, there were television commentators and journalists who advocated that Ian Botham should be captain, and that is what was decided.

The selection of Botham aped what was considered to be the Australian principle – the best player, the one person sure of his place in the side, make him captain. The problem was that although Botham has perhaps given more delight than any other cricketer over the past 20 years, the qualities he possesses are not those suited for captaincy. 'Natural' and 'instinctive' are the epithets most used about him, but the instinctiveness is that of the boy who says to his mates, 'Come on, lads, let's go scrumping', and climbs the wall into the orchard without looking back to see if anyone is behind him.

Exuberant in all he does, his every action demanding a response, Botham was never likely to be a calm, thoughtful tactician. His bowling changes seldom suggested reasoned thought. His field-settings, notably for Underwood against West Indies at Lord's, could be horrendous. There was also the suggestion that his 'natural' approach to the game did not always allow him a complete grasp of events. An opponent gave the final match of the 1984 season, Somerset v Nottinghamshire, as evidence of this.

Nottinghamshire needed to win this game to deprive Essex of the title. To his credit, Botham played the game without thought of external influences. His declaration on the last afternoon left Notts to make 297 with 52 overs of the day to be played. What Botham's critics insist is that he did not realise that, irrespective of the number of overs that had been bowled, 20 overs still had to be bowled in the last hour. In the event, with two spinners operating for most of the innings,

Captaincy proved not to be Ian Botham's strong point.

Notts had 60 overs in which to reach their target. They failed, being bowled out for 293 with two balls of the match remaining. In Botham's defence, such niceties as number of overs have not interested him greatly. His prime concern has been for the joy in the game and the sense of physical elation that it gives.

He captained England in twelve Tests, nine against West Indies, three against Australia. Eight were drawn, four were lost. In the West Indies, he also had to contend with the tragic and sudden death of his assistant manager, the much liked and respected Ken Barrington, and with the Guyanese refusal to allow Robin Jackman to play in their country because of his South African connections. His twelve Tests as England captain were played against the two strongest Test-playing sides, fielding their strongest available sides. Nine of these Tests were against the West Indies against whom Mike Brearley never led an England side, and three against Australia to whom Brearley, when confronted by the strongest opposition, had lost all three Tests. Before the ultimate condemnation of Botham, these are points worth considering.

What cannot be argued, however, is that when he was captain of England Botham's own performances with bat and ball fell away dramatically. Having been dismissed for a 'pair' at Lord's in the second Test against Australia in 1981, he resigned the England captaincy. The press had been baying for his blood, and he gave the impression that he felt that the world was against him. England were one Test down in the series.

Who would now lead England? There was no obvious candidate. Gooch was not yet confident enough in his own position. Boycott was unacceptable to the majority although bewilderingly miscast as the people's leader in some quarters. Willis was the honest workman; Gower a distant young pretender. It was the classical political situation where the *éminence grise* is called from retirement in the hour that his country needs him most. Brearley returned, after some persuasion, and led England to one of the greatest and most thrilling of triumphs, winning three of the last four Tests.

Botham was a changed cricketer. He played innings of such power and devastation at Headingley and Old Trafford that memory of them still warms the heart. At Headingley, Bob Willis produced a spell of bowling as passionate as any seen on a cricket field, and Australia, needing a mere 130 to win, were beaten by 18 runs.

Brearley's contributions with the bat were of little significance. He was the first English cricketer for a generation to be selected for the Test side for his qualities as a captain alone.

His first asset was what we might call an 'amateur' one which John Arlott was quick to recognise. 'The great thing about you, Mike, is that you're the only England captain who knows it doesn't *really* matter.' Armed with this detachment, Brearley was able to bring a calm and calculating authority to the game. He allied this to a uncompromising professional approach to cricket which bordered on the ruthless. His stubborn refusal to give way on the point of taking Roger Tolchard, an inferior wicket-keeper, to Australia in 1978–79, caused John Murray to resign as a Test selector. He insisted that Alan Knott return to the England side when he took over again in 1981, and the faithful Bob Taylor was dropped. He was excited by debate with his own players, arguing forcibly with Emburey and others over field-settings. Edmonds, a rebellious spirit, alone remained unconvinced by his reasoning and his persuasive charm, yet against Edmonds one must set the fact that Botham and Boycott, whom others found it difficult to handle, were at their best under Brearley. One reason could be that Brearley fought hard for his men and for their rights, financial and social. Indeed, one criticism levelled against him was that in his time the England team became a closed shop and attitudes were mercenary.

As a figure-head, he offended some northern sensibilities. There was too much of the assured, urbane south about him, and he was booed when he went out to bat for Middlesex at Headingley, yet this was as grotesque a mistake as to believe that Boycott was the people's champion. Brearley was lured back to cricket, willing to take over the captaincy of Middlesex, because he was fascinated by the workings of the human mind. His concern was for people rather than cricket, and that was his strength.

He saw cricket as a skilful game, played with real people and demanding intelligent manipulation. For an intellect such as his, it was an irresistible challenge.

The detachment, the skill and charm with people, the intelligent and probing mind, these are all admirable qualities for a captain, but they are of little use if the man has no knowledge of the game itself. A fact that is often ignored is that Brearley's knowledge and understanding of cricket were profound. Never was this more clearly shown than when he captained Middlesex at Lord's for the last time in August 1982.

Surrey were the visitors, and when Brearley looked at the wicket he was convinced that it was so worn that it would take spin on the last afternoon and that a side would not make 150 on it. So sure was he of this fact that he asked the 50 year old Fred Titmus to play as an extra spinner.

Middlesex batted laboriously, rain interrupted play, and when Surrey declared at lunch time on the last day only three runs separated the sides. Middlesex then hit briskly, and, to the astonishment of all, Brearley declared, leaving Surrey 135 minutes in which to make 161. It was a declaration that seemed to have presented Surrey with the match, for, in spite of Brearley's pre-match assertion and his inclusion of Titmus, only five wickets in the match had so far fallen to the spinners.

Brearley's reading of the wicket proved to be correct, however, for, in spite of losing Edmonds with a strained back after he had taken three wickets, Middlesex won by 58 runs with 7.3 overs of the day still unused. It was a victory at which critics could only gasp in wonder. Brearley's county captaincy career was to end with his fourth Championship.

In the history of cricket, no other captain can boast a record which approaches Brearley's at Test and county level. Some of them had records equally as good at one or other; none at both.

Brearley was lucky. He was lucky with the quality of his side at Middlesex, lucky to win a place in the England side in the first place, lucky to lead his country at a time when much of the opposition was weak; but he accepted his luck and used it to the full. Others have had highly talented sides and weak opposition and still failed to produce good results. Brearley was ambitious and recognised the ambition and the desires of others. He was tough and demanding, but compassionate and quick to praise. On the debit side, many would blame him for the excessive displays of congratulation which are common on the cricket field today. He was purposeful and communicative. His authority was benevolent and may even have been tinged with vanity, but one can only look on his record with awe and admiration.

10 Winning – the Cause for Concern

As Brearley left the Test and county scene in triumph, the question reasserted itself as to who would now lead. Gatting, almost by default, took over at Middlesex who continued to prosper while Keith Fletcher was asked to lead England to India and Sri Lanka in the winter of 1981–82.

Fletcher was 37 years old and had not played Test cricket for over four years, his last encounters being in the less affluent times. He had been a Test batsman of high quality, a point not always recognised, a county cricketer for 19 years and captain of Essex seven years. Under his leadership, Essex had won their first honours in more than 100 years of existence and become, along with Middlesex, the most formidable side in the country. On the county circuit it was generally accepted that he had no equal as a captain, that he was superior even to Brearley and that only Jim Watts of Northamptonshire, a quietly effective leader of a moderate side, could compare with him.

Fletcher's upbringing had been hard. He was one of Brian Taylor's men who had seen Essex through the financially lean years of the 1960s, and he had been scarred by events. His Test début at Headingley in 1968 epitomised much that he was to suffer. He was dismissed without scoring, missed two difficult chances at slip and was barracked by a Yorkshire crowd who thought their own man, Phil Sharpe, should have been in the side. Essentially a country boy and a private person, he could never provide the press or the media with the ostentation which was their diet, and he was not well treated by them in his early days. Their treatment marked him, and he had tended to withdraw into himself and his team.

At Essex, Fletcher was known as the shrewdest of tacticians and a man whose attitudes were uncompromising in the demands he made

The acclaim. Keith Fletcher and Ken McEwan after Essex had won the John Player League Trophy, 1985.

of his side. He was a professional of the old school, street-wise, and he quickly stamped his own personality on a group of lively professionals with whom he had grown up.

The county circuit is an intimate circle. There is rivalry and companionship. Strengths and weaknesses are known, no quarter is given, but players are linked by the knowledge that they are of a select band, small in number, who are privileged to be paid for something that they enjoy doing. Within this close community, Keith Fletcher was, and is, a highly respected leader of men. A tour to India presented different problems.

In England, he and his opposing county skippers generally had an understanding of each other and knew how a game would be played. In India, where Gavaskar, like his successor Kapil Dev, while worshipped as a player, lived his life as captain with the sword of Damocles suspended over him, there could be no meeting point between the two captains. The resultant series, which England lost, was one of tedium. Neither was Fletcher's cause helped by the cloak and dagger preparations that were being conducted to set up the rebel tour to South Africa. On his return to England, Fletcher was

The Benson and Hedges World Championship of Cricket, 1985, Melbourne. Gavaskar, the Indian captain, holds the trophy. A few months later he was deposed.

summarily and ungraciously dismissed from the Test captaincy. At county level, his success continued unabated.

One former England captain put forward the idea that Fletcher was not the man to lead a *touring* side, that the type of man that they needed in India was somebody like Mark Nicholas of Hampshire. Hampshire, after an interlude in which West Indian Roy Marshall and ex-Derbyshire wicket-keeper Bob Stephenson led the side, have tended to preserve public school traditions on the south coast. Nick Pocock was struggling to be worthy of a place in the side when he was captain, but Nicholas has proved an energetic, likeable and enthusiastic county skipper whose batting has fallen short of Test standard, much to the regret, one feels, of those in authority who had dreams of another Brearley. Interestingly, the Hampshire Hogs, an influential and prestigious club within the county, claim that all but two of the men who have captained Hampshire have been Hogs. Not surprisingly, the two are Marshall and Stephenson.

The suggestion that Fletcher was not the man to lead an England side to India, although he was the best captain in the country, implied that what he lacked was not cricketing expertise, but the social graces demanded in meeting the media and local dignitaries. The ghost of Warner still stalks.

Following the dismissal of Fletcher, the selectors turned to Bob Willis who had been the England vice-captain. A man passionately dedicated to the England cause who had somehow kept himself in the game when injury and wear and tear suggested that he should retire, Willis remains a strange choice as captain. Long service, faithfulness and endeavour are admirable attributes, but they hardly constitute the sole requirements of a captain.

He had taken over at Warwickshire following some dissension over the captaincy of Whitehouse who was rather shabbily treated. There had been revival at Edgbaston when the John Player League had beeen won in 1980, but Warwickshire cricket had generally continued to lumber along. The problem that faced Willis as captain of Warwickshire was the same as that which had faced Fletcher at Essex in 1972 and Gooch at the same county some 14 years later, the demands at international level were so great that there was little time to spare for the county.

In 1979 Bob Willis, bolstered by five wickets against Kent on the last afternoon of the season, took *eleven* first-class wickets for Warwickshire at 36.45 runs each. In three Tests for England the same summer, he took ten wickets, and he also played for England in the World Cup. On one occasion, when he was captain of Warwickshire and came on to bowl, a voice from the crowd enquired, 'Bowler's name?'

Bob Willis directs.

Willis made himself into one of the world's great fast bowlers and, for a long time, carried the England attack on his shoulders, so that preservation of his powers and fitness were important but hardly conducive to success or good public relations at county level. The factors which made him a great fast bowler, the single-minded endeavour and the almost trance-like quality of his application, were scarcely likely to be helpful in leading a side, making calculated decisions and astute bowling changes. He was a rouser, but on the field he too often retreated into some remote jungle of his own mind and left his bowlers to get on with it.

A captain, like a teacher, cannot exert influence beyond the limits of his own inhibitions.

Willis gave way to Gower, and Gower, as we have seen, committed the sin of leading England in two series against West Indies. Like Denness, he was unlucky in his timing. In the same season that he lost the England captaincy, Gower was also relieved of the captaincy of Leicestershire. The county had won the Benson and Hedges Cup under Gower in 1984, but departures and resignations and the failure to fulfil potential brought his stewardship to an end. Success was the only measure. A most likeable and charming young man who said that he was still learning the job of captaincy but who, like the football manager, had not learned quickly enough. Willey, tough, determined, uncompromising, succeeded. He would dragoon Leicestershire into shape.

Significantly, with the deposition of Gower and the resignation of Gooch, by the end of the 1987 season, only Gatting among the 17 county captains was a current Test player, and Gatting himself was having problems.

His first Test as captain against India at Headingley had ended in defeat. His leadership had been nervous, fidgety, with constant changes in field-placings suggesting unease, and bowlers not used at the ends which would have helped them more. In the second Test as captain, against India at Edgbaston. England were 0 for 2. Gatting could have been out to his first scoring stroke and should have been out to his second. He snicked a ball from Chetan Sharma catchably between first slip and the wicket-keeper. Gavaskar and More obstructed each other and the chance was lost. Gatting went on to score 183 not out. He was named as captain for the rest of the summer, but one wonders what the selectors, who said that they made him captain because of his positive approach, would have done if Gatting had been caught for four as he should have been. The series against New Zealand was lost, but the triple triumph in Australia followed.

It was the following summer, 1987, that things began to go wrong. Middlesex's run of success had continued under Gatting, but after the Benson and Hedges Cup victory in 1986 the county lost its way. The 1987 season was their worst for nearly 20 years. There were suggestions, even in the serious dailies, that it might be better to make Gatting club captain at Middlesex and let Emburey or someone else lead the side on the field, for defeat by Pakistan at Headingley meant that England lost their third home series in succession. Gatting's comments to the press, affable in victory, were greeted with less enthusiasm in defeat. A clearer, more analytical argument was looked for than the 'Things went against us'.

To reach the World Cup Final in India and Pakistan was an achievement far better than most had expected, particularly as neither Botham nor Gower had been available for the competition, but trouble struck as soon as England began their tour of Pakistan following the World Cup.

Historical factors and the refusal of the TCCB to withdraw David Constant from the panel of Test umpires the previous year had roused Pakistani indignation. England Test sides in Pakistan have never been noted for diplomacy and sensitivity, neither has the English press and media, and the Pakistani anger was now fuelled by the reactions of England players to the umpires' decisions in the first Test match which Pakistan won handsomely. A few years earlier, in India, Gower had suffered some dreadful decisions, but he had ordered his men to display no adverse reaction to an umpire's verdict, insisting that he would attend to all grievances and complaints in private with the Indian Board. England won the series. Gatting's approach was very different. He gave obvious signs that he disapproved of being given out leg before when sweeping, although many would agree with the umpire's verdict, and Broad had to be ushered from the wicket by Gooch after he had been given out, wrongly, caught behind. The lack of tact, interpreted in a proud country as insults to the nation, erupted when Gatting and Shakoor Rana, the umpire, engaged in a verbal battle at the end of the second day of the second Test match. Rana accusing Gatting of cheating when he moved a fielder with a wave of the hand as Hemmings was running in to bowl.

The umpire refused to take the field on the third day until he had received a written apology which Gatting finally gave at the insistence of the TCCB. The England captain apologised for his use of bad language, but he received no apology from the Pakistan umpire who, it was affirmed, had also used bad language and was in the wrong in his action.

Initially, the cricket world was divided, although very few condoned the arguing with the umpire as presented by both Broad and Gatting. Later, however, after Gatting had been ordered to apologise and seemingly left stranded by those in authority, the England captain was seen as a martyr. Gatting was cast in the role of the working-class Englishman with the London accent and a professional rather than an old-style amateur background who had been betrayed by the gentlemen of Lord's. It was a dangerous half-truth.

That Gatting was provoked by the treatment he and his side received in Pakistan was undeniable. That he was an unwitting pawn in a political game which had its roots in the history of the British Empire was also undeniable. The top TCCB officials, Raman Subba Row and Alan Smith, flew to Pakistan to ensure that the final Test would go ahead and to reassure Gatting and his side that they had the understanding and backing of the Board. Support for Gatting as captain of England was reaffirmed, yet doubts lingered.

However successful Gatting had been in Australia, he had lost to

The trials of captaincy – Mike Gatting.

Pakistan at Headingley, displayed feverish traits in his batting in the World Cup and had shown a lack of control in the most sensitive cricket-playing country in the world. Was he really the man to lead England on tour?

Gatting was abrasive but honest, tactically limited but transparently true in endeavour. Memories of the Falklands were evoked in the popular press. Yet even the Falklands victory left its dead and wounded, and there was a suspicion in many minds that Gatting might end as one of the victims of the expedition to Pakistan. At the insistence of the Prime Minister, he had been named on the Honours List for leading England to victory in Australia, but by the beginning of the 1988 season that success was still the limit of his achievement. His faults had become obvious, not least of them his weaknesses in communication and diplomacy. Australia, 1986–87, seemed a very long way away.

Through the labyrinth of finance and passion which constitutes the modern game, the counties search for someone to lead them. Gloucestershire and Worcestershire chose quiet, thoughtful men never likely to be caught up in the whirl of international cricket. Both were helped in their task by external events.

At Gloucestershire, David Graveney faced the severest criticism and cries for his dismissal as the County, in the post-Procter and Zaheer period, wallowed. Execution was stayed, and Gloucestershire signed a little-known West Indian paceman, Courtney Walsh. Walsh took more than 100 wickets, and suddenly Gloucestershire were in contention for honours. Crowds flocked back to Bristol, and David Graveney was heaped with praise. Was this likeable, courteous man a better captain than he had been? Or was it simply that Curran, Walsh and the advance of Lawrence had made Gloucestershire a better side?

Phil Neale at Worcestershire, an equally likeable and courteous man, led his side to two knock-out semi-finals in 1986, but they were beaten in both. The following season, with Botham and Dilley now on the staff, they won the Sunday League and membership doubled.

Surrey, in search of former glories, persuaded Ian Greig to return from Australia and to first-class cricket as captain in 1987. It was an appointment that took the cricket world by surprise, but Surrey had seemed rudderless for some years and they saw in Greig the man who would restore pride, passion, discipline, commitment and, thereby, success. Greig's early impact on the side would suggest that Surrey chose wisely and had researched their man well.

Somerset, too, had been faced with disintegration and, in spite of the sixes of Botham and Richards, were failing lamentably in all competitions. Internal strife came to an end with the non-retention of

Viv Richards and the departure of Botham. Peter Roebuck, firm, intelligent, almost austere, was put in charge to restore order.

Phil Carrick, with Boycott no longer in the side and disunion at an end, quietly and effectively took Yorkshire to victory in the Benson and Hedges Cup, while David Hughes recalled the heady days of Jack Bond at Old Trafford as he led Lancashire to second place in the County Championship in 1987. But the title was won by Nottinghamshire, who were captained by South African Clive Rice.

An all-rounder of the very highest quality, Clive Rice was selected for South Africa's tour of Australia in 1971–72. The tour was cancelled, and Rice was never to play Test cricket. South Africa's excommunication from international cricket inevitably limited the opportunities of young players like Rice so that when Ramsbottom, the Lancashire League club, offered him a contract for the 1973 season he eagerly accepted.

He proved to be an outstanding all-rounder in the League, but he had no thought of playing county cricket until approached by Jack Bond, the former Lancashire captain who had become manager of Nottinghamshire. Bond asked Rice to come to Trent Bridge to replace the departing Gary Sobers.

The challenge of following Sobers was one that Rice could not resist. Great player as he was, Sobers had failed to lift Notts in the manner that had been hoped. Rice's arrival brought instant improvement, but in spite of his magnificent personal contribution, Notts cricket remained close to a shambles. The county committee realised this and appointed Rice captain in 1978. Before he could take over, however, his involvement with Packer's World Series cricket was revealed. In the general hysteria that greeted the news of Packer's venture, Rice was stripped of the captaincy and Smedley restored. Happily for Notts, they also signed Richard Hadlee, so that they now had two of the best all-round cricketers in the world.

In circumstances that did little credit to the Club, Smedley was relieved of the captaincy of Nottinghamshire. The announcement came as Notts were beating Gloucestershire at Trent Bridge shortly before the side left for Edgbaston for the second round of the Gillette Cup match with Warwickshire. The reason given was that it was felt that Notts needed a 'different type of personality' as captain. The new captain was Clive Rice.

However badly the affair had been managed, the appointment of Rice as captain was an inspirational move. In 1980, Notts finished third in the Championship, the highest position that they had occupied for 51 years. The following year they won the title. In 1984, they were denied the Championship only in the last over of the season, and in 1982 and 1985, they were losing finalists at Lord's. Rice's finale

A profound influence on Nottinghamshire cricket ending in the triumphs of 1987 – Clive Rice.

for Notts was to lead them to another County Championship and victory in a magnificent NatWest Trophy Final in 1987, the season he stated would be his last.

Clive Rice never captured the flamboyant publicity that attended Sobers or Botham, yet his record at Notts was infinitely better than that of Sobers and he won the Silk Cut all-rounder competition three years in succession with Botham trailing. Had he been able to play Test cricket, it is likely that his achievements would have outshone those of Mike Brearley. He led South Africa to success against 'rebel' sides, and, under him, Transvaal dominated South African cricket, winning everything that was available to win for two seasons and only once relinquishing their hold on the Currie Cup.

A polite and gentle man, Clive Rice has passed through county cricket and only towards the end has received the praise and attention that he has deserved. He is a man whose approach to the game is cool, determined, intelligent and resourceful. He is strict and demanding in leadership and despairs of those who are complacent and lacking in endeavour. He omitted Derek Randall when he felt that the England batsman had lost his commitment to the county's cause, and he attempted to sign Ian Gould when he was leaving Middlesex because he felt that Bruce French was not applying himself sufficiently. Gould moved to Sussex instead of Notts, and French practised assiduously to become England's wicket-keeper. To Broad, Robinson and Newell, Rice was of immense help, encouraging them warmly as they worked hard at their games. In his personal contribution as a player to Notts success, he produced runs and wickets and catches when they were needed most, just as Procter had done at Gloucestershire. He was tactically sharp as a captain, knowledgeable of his opponents, mindful of their strengths and weaknesses. English cricket was enriched by his presence.

Those who have tasted success as captain at Test and county level present a motley group. Is there really a common denominator that links such disparate personalities as Lord Hawke, Percy Chapman, Brian Sellers, Stuart Surridge, Walter Robins, Douglas Jardine, Mike Brearley, Keith Fletcher, Leonard Green, Jack Bond and Clive Rice? And were they totally in control of events that brought success?

We have noted how Brian Close had little influence on what happened when England beat West Indies at The Oval in 1966, and Mike Brearley has related how, in the dramatic Headingley Test of 1981, he wanted Willis to bowl uphill and it was only at the request of Willis himself, with the backing of Botham and Taylor, that he switched him to the end from which he gave England's outstanding bowling performance in recent Test history and won his side an improbable victory. Had Gower been able to spend his entire career captaining England against a moderate Australian side in England instead of having to go off and face the West Indies at their most hostile, would he have been acclaimed as a great leader? Clive Lloyd's period as captain of West Indies at the peak of their achievement has endowed him with greatness in the minds of many, yet others would hold his weakness as a disciplinarian responsible for a decline in manners and behaviour which has sullied the game in the past decade. How do we measure our leaders?

Doug Insole, one of the wise men of cricket administration and a fine captain in his day, has described cricket captaincy as a combination of 'nursemaid, diplomat, politician, accountant, Public Relations Officer, meteorologist, and horticultural consultant'. We know that a man adept at all these things is not common on this earth, so rather we must accept that a good captain is one who finds himself in the right place at the right time as did Winston Churchill, on a more important plain, in the years between 1940 and 1945, but not thereafter. Brearley was right for Middlesex and England at the end of the 1970s and in the early 1980s, but one can never imagine him as a captain of Yorkshire. Fletcher's innate wisdom and his knowledge of the game tried and tested by a harsh apprenticeship brought Essex to a height that they had never before attained, but in a Sussex or Somerset side of the 1930s he might well have been omitted in July and August to make way for the amateurs.

We are guilty of investing our captains with ideals and qualities which they would not claim for themselves because we need the comfort of belief and trust in them. When they do not fulfil our dreams we are quick to cast them down. We grow impatient for what we look upon as success, for in an age of materialism this has become the only yardstick. Those who played with both will tell you that Jim Watts was a better captain than Mike Brearley, but, as Northants won only the Benson and Hedges Cup and Watts never played for England, there are very few people who would accept that judgment.

There is a depressing over-simplification when it comes to judgments on the art of captaincy; those who win are deemed good; those who lose are deemed bad. The responsibilities and duties of leadership, like the game itself, are more complex than that. They demand an understanding of and a sympathy for people, a manipulation of minds and instincts, a sense of authority that will be quick to decide and to act, and a self-control that will be an example to others. Such qualities deserve our deepest consideration and respect for they still represent a hope for the preservation of ethical standards, of calm and sensitivity, in a world where people have come to accept exaggeration and success at any price as the norm.

A comparative table of 31 Test captains and their percentage of success, allowing two points for a win and one for a draw to tie.

The Test match in which the captain first led his side to victory is numbered on the right.

	Tests as Captain	W.	D.	L.	Tie	%	
D.G. Bradman (Australia)	24	15	6	3		75.00	3
J.M. Brearley (England)	31	18	9	4		72.58	2
A.L. Hassett (Australia)	24	14	6	4		70.83	1
I.M. Chappell (Australia)	30	15	10	5		66.66	3
C.H. Lloyd (West Indies)	74	36	26	12		66.21	1
L. Hutton (England)	23	11	8	4		65.21	1
R. Benaud (Australia)	28	12	11	4	1	64.28	1
W.M. Woodfull (Australia)	25	14	4	7		64.00	2
P.B.H. May (England)	41	20	11	10		62.19	1
R. Illingworth (England)	31	12	14	5		61.76	1
G.S. Chappell (Australia)	48	21	14	13		58.33	1
M.C. Cowdrey (England)	27	8	15	4		57.40	1
J. Darling (Australia)	21	7	10	4		57.14	2
G.P. Howarth (New Zealand)	30	11	12	7		56.66	1
M.J.K. Smith (England)	25	5	17	3		54.00	6
E.R. Dexter (England)	30	9	14	7		53.33	1
W.R. Hammond (England)	20	4	13	3		52.50	4
J.D. Goddard (West Indies)	22	8	7	7		52.27	1
W.M. Lawry (Australia)	25	9	8	8		52.00	1
S.M. Gavaskar (India)	41	11	20	10		51.00	1
R.B. Simpson (Australia)	39	12	15	12		50.00	1
A.H. Kardar (Pakistan)	23	6	11	6		50.00	2
G. St. A. Sobers (West Indies)	39	9	20	10		48.71	1
R.N. Kapil Dev (India)	34	4	22	7	1	45.58	21
M.W. Gatting (England)	15	2	9	4		43.33	6
B.S. Bedi (India)	22	6	5	11		38.63	5
Mansur Ali Khan (India)	40	9	12	19		37.50	10
A.C. MacLaren (England)	22	4	7	11		34.09	1
K.J. Hughes (Australia)	28	4	11	13		33.92	1
D.I. Gower (England)	26	5	7	14		32.69	11
J.R. Reid (New Zealand)	34	1	13	18		27.94	3

Complete until the end of the English season, 1987.
After the tour to New Zealand, Gatting's percentage had dropped to 28.57.

Index